Around The Majors in 60 Days

My Baseball Dream

Ray Bergman

Ray Bergman

with Judith Hettler

Foster City, California

Photographs of stadiums courtesy of
Paul Munsey and Cory Suppes
www.ballparks.com
Reproduced with permission.

Book design, layout, and printing by
Falcon Books, San Ramon, California

ISBN 0-9658970-0-1

Cambridge Advisory Services, Inc.
1155 Chess Drive
Suite 100
Foster City, CA 94404

Toll Free
1-888-91DREAM
1-888-913-7326

Table of Contents

Acknowledgements

I want to express my utmost appreciation to my best friend and collaborator, Judith Hettler, who took my mundane facts and brought them to life with her artistry. She was instrumental in writing this manuscript.

My heartfelt gratitude must be extended to my son Marc, without whose participation and encouragement through some tough times this dream would not have been fulfilled.

I especially appreciate the help and support provided by my good friend Barry Keast throughout the journey. Special thanks to Munsey and Suppes for providing "my baseball dream" with coverage on their web site, www.ballparks.com. I want to thank Judith Perkins and Kate St. Germain for editing the manuscript, and Diane Gibson of the Avis Corporation (Oakland Airport) for renting me a brand new car. I am also grateful to many of the Major League Baseball franchises who provided me with complimentary passes and other perks.

And there were those who provided support and encouragement along the way—I want to thank them all: My cousin Madeline, Uncle Sam, Ben Robert, my parents Edith and Adolph, brother Abby and sister-in-law Rose, my nephew Jonathan, Aunt Evelyn, Peter, Robbi and Eli, John Peterson, the Perskys, the Mariners, the Clines, the DeDeckers, Ken Goldman, Jenny O'Connor, and Ron and Emory Klein.

The Beginning

It is 3:15 in the afternoon on Friday, July 26th, and my front door bell is ringing. It's my friend Barry who asks me if I'm ready to go. I quickly reply, "You bet I am!" I have waited and planned for this day for over six months and it has finally arrived.

This is the start of a long-planned odyssey. I intend to travel to all of the major league baseball stadiums in North America, witnessing a game in each and every ballpark, bringing you observations on baseball in particular and the journey along the way. This will involve some 15,000 miles, 28 stadiums, 2 countries and a 60 day time schedule, give or take a few days.

My goal is to complete this venture in a very tight time frame. Juggling game dates and coordinating them with miles of geography are the main challenges.

I have chosen to travel via automobile. I know this isn't the fastest or the easiest way to go for the amount of time I have allotted, but it is, I feel, the best way to really see, smell and touch the heart of this great game of baseball. And, as an extra gift, experience some of the heart of America.

My name is Ray Bergman and I love baseball. My love of the game began when I was a very small boy. To this day, I can still vividly remember holding onto my father's hand as we walked into the Polo Grounds on a warm summer's day. I can, with almost no effort, smell the odors of the old ballpark—the freshly cut grass, the smell of roasted peanuts and hot dogs meant only for hungry little boys like me—and the sounds! The noise of the crowd was like thunder that roared in my ears—and the wonderful cracking sound of the bat as it connected with the ball. What heaven for a child!

I'm grown up now, the Polo Grounds is no more, and I've long since given up most of that little boy's dreams. But there is one dream I have never let go of: to make my small contribution to baseball and to pay homage to the game I love.

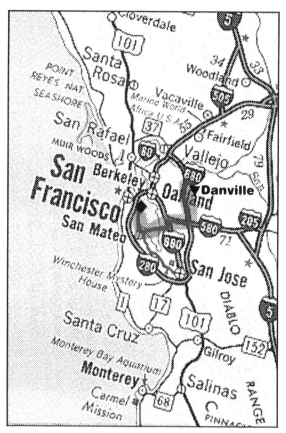

Danville to San Francisco via I-680, I-580, I-880, SR92 and US101.

CHAPTER I

San Francisco—3-Com Park
(Formerly known as Candlestick Park)

As I close the front door I glance at the thermometer on my porch. It reads 97 degrees. We are, of course, wearing summer clothing. It's a forty mile drive due west from my home in the East Bay to the "Stick" on the San Francisco peninsula. For each mile we drive the temperature will drop by about one degree. We are prepared for the phenomenon that lies ahead, for summer literally turning into winter. Therefore, both of us have brought our cold weather gear of sweatshirts and parkas. We know how a summer's night in the stadium can chill your bones.

Before heading across the bay, we'll pick up my rental car from the local Avis agency. I'll be using this car for the entire trip of the Major League Baseball Challenge (MLBC). Avis was kind enough to provide me with a new Dodge Intrepid with just 447 miles on the odometer.

As we reach the top span of the San Mateo Bridge, linking the East Bay with the peninsula, we see a magnificent view. A DC-10 is overhead as it makes its final approach to San Francisco airport. The fog bank engulfs the hills and the "City by the Bay" is in full view as are the airport and the baseball stadium.

As I drive north on US Highway 101, I remember my mother telling me about the day I was born. That March morning in 1942 had indeed blown in like a lion. Although late in the month, there was enough snow, sleet and wind to remind New York that winter had not yet let go. I came into this world at the Bronx Maternity Hospital, the location being important to my story only because of its proximity to the fabled "House That Ruth Built", Yankee Stadium. My course had been plotted. I was clearly fated to live my life under the influence of the game of baseball.

Let's take a look at baseball back then and see how it has evolved. In 1942, Major League Baseball was structured as follows:

- There were two leagues—the American and National.
- Each league had eight teams.
- The schedule consisted of a 154 game season.
- Each team played one another 22 games (11 at home and 11 away) each season.
- There was no inter-league play except for the World Series.

National League	American League
Boston Braves	Boston Red Sox
Brooklyn Dodgers	Chicago White Sox
Chicago Cubs	Cleveland Indians
Cincinnati Redlegs	Detroit Tigers
New York Giants	New York Yankees
Philadelphia Phillies	Philadelphia Athletics
Pittsburgh Pirates	St. Louis Browns
St. Louis Cardinals	Washington Senators

We arrive at the "Stick" an hour before game time. Before leaving the parking lot we don our sweatshirts, with hoods ready for deployment, and put on our winter jackets. It's the middle of summer, 57 degrees and counting down as the fog rolls in.

The Giants franchise actually began in New York City in 1883. The team was then called the New York Gothams. In 1886, the name was changed to the Giants. They played their home games at the Polo Grounds through the 1957 season. This ballpark had very short dimensions down each foul line and then expanded rapidly to one of the deepest center field areas in baseball, some 483 feet from home plate at its furthest point.

In 1958, the Giants broke the hearts of millions of New York fans, including mine, when they packed their bags and moved to San Francisco, about as far west as a team could go to play major league baseball and still remain on the continent. The first two seasons on the west coast the games were played in Seal Stadium, a small minor league ballpark south of the downtown hub of the city. In 1960, the team moved to the newly completed Candlestick Park in an area of the city jutting out into the western edge of San Francisco Bay. Known as Candlestick Point because of its long pointed shape, it was one of the least desirable areas in the city due to the cold fog and wind. In fact, it became famous for its blowing wind when it blew Stu Miller off the pitchers' mound during the 1961 Allstar Game.

Originally the outfield was open to the bay but later the entire stadium was enclosed. Today, Candlestick (3-Com Park) is a two level stadium with luxury suites between the lower and upper levels. There is a bleacher section in left field and a pavilion area in right. The stadium is completely enclosed with stands, seats and virtually no open areas.

Candlestick Park was the site for Game 3 of the 1989 World Series between the Oakland A's and the Giants, known as the Bay Bridge

World Series. Just thirty minutes before game time, an earthquake rocked the Bay Area and put the Series on hold for ten days until the ballpark was pronounced safe for play.

The Giants have plans for a new stadium in an area of downtown called China Basin in the year 2000. Its kinder and gentler weather is one of the major reasons for the move. Another factor is that public transportation will be a lot more accessible at the new location.

The franchise has won 19 National League pennants and 5 World Series titles, their last coming in 1954 when they swept the Cleveland Indians four straight. They have been to two other World Series since then, in 1962 and again in 1989, but have not come away with the grand prize of baseball.

We have time to taste the highly recommended forty clove garlic chicken sandwich. It lives up to its reputation as we seem to have empty seats all around us. Just before game time the elements really take over. The wind is blowing so hard that I have to shorten the strap on my baseball cap or risk losing it. The fog continues to drift in and out and the temperature continues to fall. Our hoods are now fully deployed. To quote Mark Twain, "The coldest winter I ever spent was a summer in San Francisco."

Tonight's game is between the Atlanta Braves and my San Francisco Giants. Tom Glavine starts for the Braves against Mark Leiter for the Giants. The game turns out to be a low scoring affair highlighted by four sparkling defensive plays. Marquis Grissom hits a two-run home run over the right field fence in the top half of the sixth inning to put Atlanta in front 2-1, a lead they never relinquished. The game takes two hours and fifty-four minutes to play before a crowd of 17,540 loyal stalwarts.

After the game we head home, shedding clothing as we again go from season to season. This will be my last night in my own bed for awhile. Tomorrow I will be leaving solo for Southern

California and the Milwaukee Brewers/California Angels game in Anaheim on Sunday.

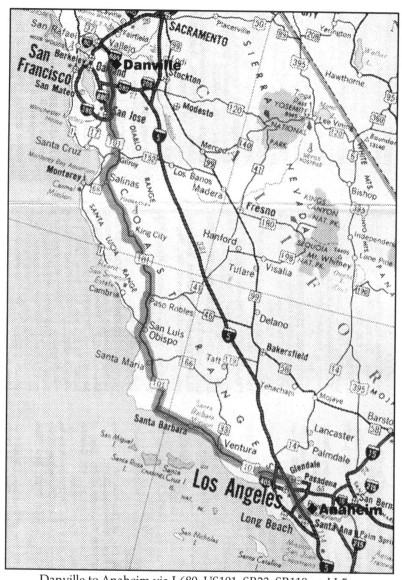

Danville to Anaheim via I-680, US101, SR23, SR118 and I-5.

CHAPTER II

Anaheim—Anaheim Stadium (The Big 'A')

It takes me several hours to pack and load the car this morning. Since I'll be away from home for about two months, and I'll spend most of my time in the car, this requires some careful planning. I take a folder with maps, a small cooler, a laptop computer, golf clubs and one suitcase. Oh yes, I'm also able to find room in the trunk for my old IBM XT computer, which I'll drop off at my dad's in Florida.

It's about 450 miles to Anaheim from my home. Normally, to make the best time, I would take Interstate 5, that straight as an arrow highway which runs from Canada to Mexico. However, today being a travel day, I have extra time and will take the scenic route of US Highway 101 which winds through coastal and valley areas. It's cooler and gives the eye much more to gaze on, so I can let my thoughts wander and think about baseball and my mission.

As I pass through the East Bay foothills they are dry and golden brown. Because rain seldom falls in California between April and October we can indeed call this the "Golden State". When badly needed rain arrives sometime in mid-fall all California will turn green and spring-like. What to other states is a problem, is for us a blessing.

After traveling for only thirty minutes, I'm approaching the major interchange of I-680 and US 101 when I'm pulled over by the California Highway Patrol for speeding. Can you believe this? Not even really out of the gate yet and Smoky is greeting me with a big hello. However, all is well that ends well and after my explanation of the facts; my trip, the new car, etc., he very kindly lets me go with a "take it easy", and I'm on my way again. Or am I? It's the weekend of the Gilroy Garlic Festival and traffic is bumper-to-bumper. Forty-five minutes later I've negotiated the last of the traffic and am in the clear and sailing along. I put on the tape of *Les Miserables* and listen to my favorite, "Master of the House", as the road stretches out before me.

This route takes me through some of the most diverse real estate in California or for that matter in the country. I drive through the heart of the Salinas Valley where most of America's vegetables are grown. Next I travel along the eastern slopes of the majestic Santa Lucia coastal mountain range, and then cross over the Los Padres National Forest to the coastal cities of Pismo Beach, Santa Barbara and Ventura. The temperature, like the terrain, varies widely. The air conditioner goes on and off as I travel from inland valley to ocean. I finally head inland to Simi Valley and my cousin's house where I will spend the next few nights.

Day three, Sunday morning, July 28th, my cousin and I leave for Anaheim Stadium. It will take us about an hour and a half. Our route passes through one of the most congested areas in the country, my welcome to Los Angeles.

The California Angels were one of the earliest expansion teams in Major League Baseball (hereafter to be referred to as MLB), becoming a franchise in 1961. This was MLB's first attempt at expansion since the turn of the century. The Angels along with the "new" Washington Senators (which replaced the "original" Senators who moved to Minnesota and became the Twins) increased the American League from eight to ten teams. In 1962, the National League followed suit by adding two teams of their own, the New York Mets and the Houston Colt 45's.

The "new" Senators refers to the second time that Washington DC has had an American League franchise. The "old" team was the original Senators, who played in DC from 1901 to 1960. After they moved to Minnesota the "new" Senators played in DC until 1971 when they moved to Texas to become the Texas Rangers in 1972. Washington DC does not have a major league baseball club today. The closest franchise is in Baltimore which is about 40 miles to the northeast.

The Angels initially played their games in Los Angeles until 1966 when they moved south to Anaheim. The franchise was owned until this year by a gentleman cowboy who spent much of his early years as a western movie star. But his first love was baseball and Gene Autry owned the Angels for many years. The franchise was recently taken over by Disney Corporation and being right next door to Disneyland is a definite plus. Gene's Angels or Halos as they are called, have three Western Division titles to their credit but have never won a pennant. Over the years they've managed to turn in winning records, bring out the fans and play solid sportsmanlike ball.

Anaheim Stadium, or the "Big A" as it is commonly referred to, is a three level stadium with luxury suites on the club or second level. When constructed in 1966 it contained just over 43,000 seats. In 1979 it was expanded to accommodate 65,000. This expansion closed in

15

the stadium and caused the giant "A" frame scoreboard, its signature, to be relocated to the parking lot.

It was April, 1946 and I was four years old when I attended my first major league baseball game. I remember my mother being pregnant with my brother. My father took me to Yankee Stadium to watch the Cleveland Indians take on the New York Yankees. I didn't know much about baseball then. I do remember several events that happened that day. When we entered that huge stadium, I recall people scrambling over a baseball that was hit into the stands. I tried to get into the middle of the fracas, but my father yanked me out by my small arms. I kept asking him where the teepees were. I figured if there were Indians there.....well, you can understand a small boy's thinking. I remember after the 5th inning screaming "Come on Bobby!" as Bobby Feller was pitching a "no-no". He did indeed wind up with a no-hitter and Cleveland beat the Yankees 1-0.

My father took me down to the dugout at the end of the game to try and get me a bat but all we were able to get was a cracked one. My father still has the program for that game. He ran into Bobby about ten years ago at an exhibition game in West Palm Beach and got Bobby to autograph the almost forty year old program. This remains one of his prize possessions.

It is a very warm day, about 95 degrees at game time. As we enter the stadium all fans are given a beach towel compliments of a local market. These come in quite handy to drape around the seats on this warm afternoon. To keep the crowd cool, the Angel cheerleaders go around and spray the patrons with water from spray bottles with little fans attached.

The game between the Brewers and Angels pits Scott Karl against Mark Langston. Both pitchers are on their game as the score is Milwaukee 3 and California 2, heading into the bottom of the ninth. Jim Edmonds delivers a pinch hit homer to tie the game at three and send it into extra innings. A long four innings later the Brewers push across the eventual winning run. The game is played in a snappy four hours and twenty-nine minutes before a paid crowd of 25,539.

My cousin gamely sat through this long hot afternoon marathon like the good sport she is. Back to Simi Valley and an off day tomorrow before I head down to Chavez Ravine on Tuesday to watch the Dodgers play the Marlins.

Simi Valley to Los Angeles via SR118, I-405, I-10 and I-5.

CHAPTER III

Los Angeles—Dodger Stadium

Monday, July 29th is an off day as I wait for the Dodgers to come back in town after their road trip. I take the opportunity to visit my uncle who lives near the beach in west Los Angeles. My uncle Sam was a big part of my sports history when I was a boy. He was an outstanding softball player and athlete. We played on the same team for several years both in Brooklyn, New York and Spring Valley, New York. He was my mentor and a constant source of inspiration to me. He played on a competitive level well into his sixties.

I leave Simi Valley on Tuesday for Los Angeles and Dodger Stadium. It's a short drive, about thirty miles southeast and takes about an hour with traffic. Tonight the Dodgers will be hosting the Florida Marlins.

I still dislike "Dem Bums", the arch rivals of the Giants. The Giants and the Dodgers have probably the fiercest rivalry in all of sports. This rivalry started in New York City, when the Giants played at the

Polo Grounds in Manhattan and the Dodgers resided at Ebbets Field (the little bandbox) in the borough of Brooklyn. These two teams really can't stand each other, and it's interesting that these two arch rivals left New York and moved to the west coast in the same year of 1958. The rivalry has continued here in California but not with the same intensity as it was in New York. However, there's still enough animosity to create excitement whenever they get together.

For me, the only redeeming feature about going to see the Dodgers play is their stadium. Dodger stadium is still one of the nicest places to watch a baseball game. It's clean, has real grass and the best "eats" in baseball. The stadium has three levels of seating in the stands and two pavilion areas, one in right center and the other in left center. Looking over the pavilion areas provides some spectacular views of the San Gabriel Mountains.

The Dodger franchise began in Brooklyn in 1890. After moving west along with the Giants in 1958, they initially played their home games in the Los Angeles Coliseum. They moved into Dodger Stadium, newly built for them, in an area called Chavez Ravine in 1962 and have played there ever since. The franchise has been very successful, both in Brooklyn and Los Angeles. The Dodgers have won 21 National League titles, more than any other National League franchise, and 6 world championships. They also have a long list of "Hall of Famers", notably Jackie Robinson, Roy Campanella, Sandy Koufax and Don Drysdale.

Since I grew up in New York, the Giants were my team and the Dodgers were the enemy. I still can remember the 1951 playoff game, for the National League pennant between the two rivals. I have never forgiven my parents who forced me to attend Hebrew school the day of that famous playoff game, the game known for "The shot that was heard around the world," Bobby Thomson's momentous home run. I can still hear the late great Russ Hodges, the Giant's lead announcer, literally yelling over and over, "the Giants win the pennant, the Giants win the pennant, the Giants win the

pennant, the Giants ...." One of life's great moments happened that day and I had to hear it on a rebroadcast later that evening!
Just yesterday the Dodgers made a major announcement which rocked the sports world. Tommy Lasorda was stepping down as manager of the Dodgers. He would remain with the team as a Vice President and consultant but would no longer be their field general. Bill Russell, the interim manager during Tommy's illness, was named to the position. Tonight's game would be the start of a new era in Dodger history. It would be the first time that Lasorda hadn't presided over a game in some twenty years.

Tommy announced his retirement to the fans, along with his farewell speech, in the stadium to which he had given his heart and soul, the same stadium where he had spent his career these twenty years. The fans responded with a two and one half minute standing ovation to this great ambassador of the game of baseball. Tommy is a colorful character and was good for the game. He was often more of a cheerleader than a manager, but you can't fault his successful record.

The game between the Dodgers and the Marlins is not played particularly well. There are too many physical and mental errors on both sides, especially for high level professional teams like these two. The Marlins jump on Dodger starter Hideo Nomo in the first inning and score two runs. The Dodgers take the lead for the first time in the eighth (4-3) on an RBI triple by Raul Mondesi. The Marlins tie the game in the ninth, at four, when Dodger closer Todd Worrel balks in the tying run. The Dodgers win the game in the tenth on a Rick Parker single that drives in the winning run.

After the game I drive south on Interstate 5 to Del Mar, a pretty little seaside town, which is one hundred miles south of Los Angeles and twenty miles north of San Diego. I'll spend the night there with a friend of mine. Tomorrow night I will be at Jack Murphy Stadium in San Diego to see the Padres play the world champion Braves.

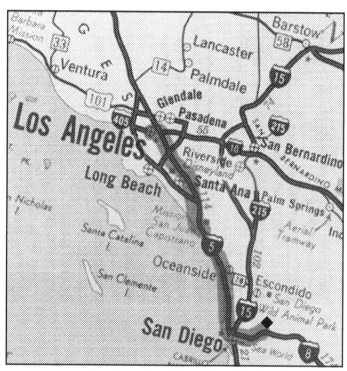

Los Angeles to San Diego via I-5 and I-8.

CHAPTER IV

San Diego—Jack Murphy Stadium

It's Wednesday, July 31st, and I've spent the morning walking the beach, looking at the boundless Pacific Ocean and thinking about the vast amount of America that lies before me. In the afternoon I sit by the pool and think about tomorrow and my son Marc flying in to meet me. Marc will be with me for the next two legs of the trip. In the evening, my friend and I drive into San Diego to watch the Padres host the Atlanta Braves.

The Padres came into the National League along with the Montreal Expos in 1969. This was the second time that the National League expanded its franchises. This brought the total strength of the majors to 24 teams, 12 in each league. Concurrent with this expansion MLB reorganized into two divisions (eastern and western) for each league. This lengthened the season since the two divisions created the need for a League Championship Series (LCS) to determine the ultimate league champion.

The Padres have produced one pennant winning team in their 26 year history, and that came in 1984 when they defeated the Chicago Cubs to claim the National League crown. They were, however, defeated in the World Series by the Detroit Tigers. They do have, arguably, the best pure hitter in baseball today, that being Tony Gwynn.

When I was five years old I started to play baseball in the school yard across from our apartment house. Our neighborhood had lots of kids, sports enthusiasts all. Most of our games were played in the streets, alongside parked cars or on the sidewalks. There weren't too many parks where kids could play in the late 1940's, in the Bronx, NYC. We didn't care; we just loved anything to do with a stick and a ball.

At the age of eight, I was one of two boys from my public school to play in the Little Leagues. They didn't give many kids the chance to play as they do now and I was the proudest kid you ever saw. I was very small for my age but played a pretty good shortstop. I was known for my fielding ability and strong arm. My "stick" unfortunately was not my strong suit.

For the next few years we conducted our own version of the Olympic Games. Our opponents were kids in the other neighborhoods. We played stickball, fast pitching-in, off the wall, box ball, slug, kick the can; we even had our own touch football contests. We weren't too particular—the game was everything. And our heads were always finding another way to hit, kick and wrestle, all the things that our richer peers never dream of doing, they with their fancy parks and expensive equipment. We didn't envy them; we wouldn't have changed places with any other human being. We were in heaven and all was right with the world!

I recall playing off the wall in the courtyard when one of my throws went into Mrs. Davis' kitchen window and right into the large pot of soup which was bubbling away on her stove. Mrs. Davis returned my best Spalding to my mother. Suffice it to say, neither lady was at all pleased.

Stickball was my favorite in those years. I was pretty good at hitting line drives and I ran like a deer. Well, at least like a deer that had to make its way between parked cars, store fronts, apartment buildings and police cars! We always needed to be aware of the cops. They drove around the neighborhoods, confiscating our bats and balls. This, of course, was largely due to the problems from the neighbors who complained about our activities on an ongoing basis. At the first inkling that the police were near, we would throw our sticks under cars, sewers or anything handy to avoid losing them to "The Law"!

The Theriot Avenue Boys, as we called ourselves, would always win the Olympics. We had the best players compared to the Parkchester Boys and the dreaded Beach Avenue Bullies. As a reward, the winning team would be able to conduct a round of "asses-up" against the losing teams. Now you didn't want to lose and I'll explain why. You see, the losers would have to bend over facing a wall, with their butts in the air and the winners would get several throws at the targets.

Stickball was my life. I lived it and breathed it. My parents, concerned about my "obsession", as they called it, started me on piano lessons. My first lesson came to a quick halt when my friends stood outside in the courtyard under my window and yelled at me to come down and play stickball. I ran like the wind, leaving the piano and my frustrated teacher forever. My parents reluctantly gave up their dream of their son becoming a musical prodigy and I was free to pursue my love of "The Game".

Let me explain briefly about these courtyards. In those days, most New York kids lived in large buildings with at least sixty to seventy family units that clustered in a "U" shape around a large open area. This was "the courtyard" and really the only large open area we had to play in. Naturally, the people living all around our "playing field" considered us kids a nuisance and life was a continual struggle between us and "them". They would yell at us to stop playing and if we didn't the excitement would start! First there would be a "shot across the bow" as we called it. This was a glass of water flying from a kitchen window. This was the warning shot and if we continued to play (which we always did), a full pail of water would be hurled at us. We really didn't mind getting soaked but the game would definitely suffer as a wet ball makes for some sloppy play. Still we played on, only to be finally stopped by darkness. "We didn't have any lights in our stadium."

Through the generosity of the San Diego Padres Public Relations Department, I was given a pass which allowed me to go on the field during batting practice and mingle with the players and coaches. I spend most of the time with the "Crime Dog" Fred McGriff. He was also kind enough to autograph my MLBC schedule and wished me a safe journey. What a thrill to stand right next to the batting cage and watch these major leaguers take their cuts!

The Padres send Bob Tweksbury to the mound to oppose Tom Glavine of the Braves. Atlanta takes advantage of Tweksbury's early wildness along with the Padres' sloppy play and scores three runs in the top of the first. The Braves continue to add to their lead one run at a time and build the score to 6-0 heading into the eighth. Glavine, who is cruising along, finally runs into trouble and the Padres put across four runs to close the gap to 6-4. The Braves add an insurance run in the ninth and Mark Wohlers closes out the Padres in the bottom half of the frame to end the game.

Marquis Grissom had four hits in five at bats and was the star of the game. There were 24,254 fans in attendance for this two hour and forty minute contest.

We drive back to Del Mar to spend the night. This completes the first leg of the MLBC. I've logged close to 800 miles and witnessed four ball games in six days. Tomorrow will be the start of the 1,300 mile drive to the next game in Arlington, Texas. I'll be heading to the San Diego airport to pick up my son who is flying in from Florida.

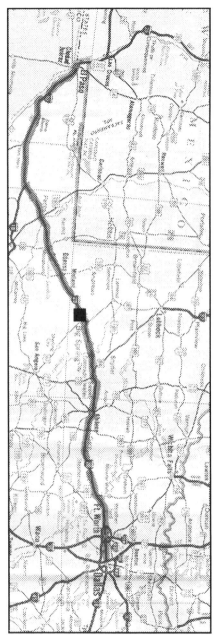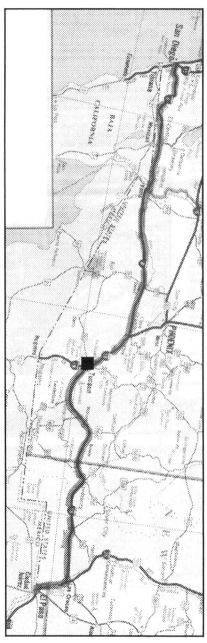

San Diego to Arlington via I-8, I-10 and I-20.

CHAPTER V

Arlington—The Ballpark at Arlington

It's Thursday, August 1st, and Marc will be arriving around 12:45. I meet his plane, right on schedule, and we promptly begin the long drive eastward on Interstate 8 for the start of leg two. Marc points out to me that he's just flown for seven hours from Miami to San Diego and without a blink we immediately start right back to where he had just come from!

Marc is twenty-five years old and an avid football fan. Baseball is too slow a game for him, but he's looking forward to the journey, the visit to the stadiums and the next eighteen days together. It will take us three days to get to our next game in Arlington, Texas. We plan to spend the night in Tucson and the following night in Big Spring, Texas before reaching Arlington and the home of the Rangers.

Today and tomorrow are travel days, no games scheduled. As we leave the coast the weather rapidly heats and very soon we've exchanged the cool green and damp air of the Pacific for the dry heat of the Southern California deserts. We can see big mountains to the east and it appears the road will never be able to get through them. We've been climbing ever since we left San Diego. We pass a nice, rather quaint looking small town called Alpine and the sign reads elevation 4,000 feet. Very shortly we descend into the desert again. That, it turns out, will be the pattern for the next day or two: high cool mountain passes and swift descents into the desert heat.

El Centro is next and the heat outside must be intense. Although we're in an air conditioned car, the glass is burning to the touch and we can see the heat waves shimmering on the sand and pavement. Next stop is Yuma, Arizona where we stop for gas and a snack. We discover it's 114 degrees and muggy, due to the effects of a monsoon over Mexico. Yuma is almost all sandy terrain and some sparse bushes scattered about. One good thing about this hot desert climate is that the allergies which I have always suffered from are completely gone. Since almost nothing grows out here, there is nothing to be allergic to!

After Yuma the road straightens dramatically and we drive it easily and fast. The posted speed limit is 75 MPH and we do all of that and more. It's a well-maintained, straight as an arrow highway and a joy to drive.

We get to Tucson at 7:30 PM, in time to enjoy a traditional southwestern dinner at the oldest restaurant in town. Tucson is an interesting combination of old and new with its modern skyscrapers and Native American influences well blended into this painted desert. We like the feeling here and a sudden late evening thunderstorm brings the temperature down to a bearable 92 degrees. After hours of major 100 plus heat, 92 feels great!

It's Friday, August 2nd, and we're two hours out of Tucson. We are really in "barren nothingness" now, the kind of place that seems to have been forgotten even by God. I would say that is a fair statement. We go through fast; the 75 mile speed limit is a particular blessing here. There's very little traffic. It's as if there were some kind of natural disaster and we are one of the few people left on earth; it's a strange feeling.

Within another half hour we're back in the mountains with lots of cactus suddenly appearing. This is the first time we've seen them on the trip and they come as sort of a surprise. It's like we should have seen them from the start. Deserts mean cactus, right? Obviously not; they're particular where they show up.

Traveling along Interstate 10, we are going through the most beautiful part of the journey up to now. As we come off the high plateau of the Continental Divide, we look down on Las Cruces, New Mexico and see this beautiful little city nestled in a fertile green valley with the jagged mountains of the San Andres range as a back drop. After the heat and the flatness of the desert, this looks like a Hollywood set of Shangri-la.

Just past Las Cruces we merge with Interstate 25 and the traffic has quite suddenly begun to thicken. We see trucks, vans, RV's and every sort of vehicle using this highway, which has access to the entire southernmost part of our country. Where they have come from we have no idea; our only guess is from Albuquerque and possibly Denver.

It's 1:30 in the afternoon and we enter the great state of Texas. We have reached the 1,600 mile mark of our journey and are just coming into El Paso. This is a huge sprawling city situated on the borders of two states and one foreign country. El Paso is the half way point of today's trip and we decide it is a good place to stop for lunch and to gas up.

As we continue eastbound the interstate parallels the Rio Grande River for about fifty miles outside of El Paso. We travel through the rolling hills of west Texas, the sky darkens and huge billows of dust shaped like funnels are dancing all around us. There is lightning and thunder and the storm is suddenly upon us. Next comes hail. Large pieces the size of golf balls hit the car like an aluminum bat hitting a baseball, and then the rain—enormous amounts of water. We pass through this entire weather system in about fifteen minutes; it is quite an experience but thankfully soon over. As quickly as it comes upon us, it leaves. The southwest is indeed a place where you can say that if you don't like the weather or the terrain, just wait a minute and it will change!

Now the skies have turned blue, all is calm and we settle down to clear perfect driving conditions. We pass into central time and lose another hour. Today is the longest day of the entire MLBC. We will cover 700 miles and cross two time zones before we're finished for the day.

Just east of Kent, Texas we leave Interstate 10 and proceed east by northeast on Interstate 20. The land changes to flat prairies covered with oil rigs and small refineries. We pull into Big Spring, our day's destination, about 10 PM. It has been a long day and we gratefully put the MLBC to bed for the night.

It's Saturday, August 3rd, and we are on our way to Arlington and the Rangers' game with the White Sox. We have a relatively short drive, a distance of about 285 miles over a landscape of gently rolling hills. The oil country is behind us. This is farm country, a place where the movie and television series of Lonesome Dove were filmed.

Arlington, the home of the Texas Rangers, is a small town community located between the megatropolis of Dallas and Fort Worth. The stadium, The Ballpark at Arlington, is designed to look old, but is one of the newest playing fields in the country, having opened only two years ago in 1994. Almost all games are played at night because of the hot Texas summers.

The Rangers came to be as a result of the second failure of major league baseball in our nation's capital, Washington, DC. The Senators' second attempt at establishing themselves in that city lasted 11 years, from 1961 through 1971. The original Senators had left DC in 1961 to go to Minneapolis and were renamed the Minnesota Twins. That same year a new franchise called the Washington Senators was created in DC. In 1972 they moved to Texas and were renamed the Texas Rangers. They played their home games at a former minor league ballpark until 1994 when they moved into the new stadium. This club has never won a pennant, either in DC or Texas. In 1996, they did, for the first time, reach post season play by winning the American League Western Division but lost to the New York Yankees in the playoffs.

When I was twelve, I was picked to be on the neighborhood sandlot baseball team. This was a great thing and definitely one of the highlights of my young life. Although I was short, I made up for it with my speed and my glove which I had worked long and hard to master. The coach gave me a big vote of confidence when I was given the left field position, the largest area to cover in the outfield. I was in heaven, but my happiness vanished when I contracted the bug known as mononucleosis and was through for the year.

During my recovery period (which seemed to last forever!), I spent a lot of time with my baby sitter, Manny Fleischer. The Fleischers lived across the hall and their son Manny was as big a nut about basketball as I was about baseball. It was with Manny that I watched my first basketball game on TV. It was between the Boston Celtics and the New York Knickerbockers or the Knicks as we call them today.

Basketball became a new interest for me. Because of the mononucleosis, I wasn't permitted to play outside, so I talked my parents into getting me a basketball hoop that hung on my bedroom door. I wasn't allowed to dribble the basketball, as our neighbor beneath us would constantly complain that "the ceiling was coming down on him!" Basketball was a different game back then, no twenty-four second clock and almost all the shooting was upward. I used to play for hours, taking shot after shot. I would create games between the professional teams of that time and imitate the star players. My favorite team was the St. Louis Hawks with Bob Petit, Clyde Lovellette and Cliff Hagin. I also admired Elgin Baylor, Oscar Robertson and Carl Braun.

I was hooked; this was my new love. Oh, it would never replace my first love. I would always be faithful to my longtime friend baseball, but basketball presented a new challenge. I must admit that for a short period of time, I neglected my stick and Spalding in favor of the hoop but I would return, I would always return to "The Game".

Marc and I have dinner at an authentic Texas type barbecue restaurant before taking the "trolley" from the motel to the ballpark. It's really a bus, but its sole function is picking up people from the various hotels and motels and taking them to the stadium. Marc is very excited, as this will be his first game. Arriving at the ballpark we are impressed with the friendliness of the fans and the cleanliness of the stadium. This is the first of the new breed of stadiums that we've encountered, and it's just beautiful. It's a three level stadium with two rows of sky boxes and luxury suites. It has real grass and several different bleacher sections. In center field there is an office building that is part of the ballpark.

The game time temperature is in the high 80's with the kind of Texas humidity that makes it fairly uncomfortable. There are lots of families with young children here tonight and overall the crowd seems excited and happy just to be here and to watch their Rangers take on the Chicago White Sox.

Kevin Gross gets the start for the Rangers as does Luis Andujar for the Sox. Chicago jumps out to an early lead by scoring four runs in the top of the first. The Rangers are playing very sloppily while Andujar and company are on cruise control, leading 8-2 going into the bottom of the seventh. The Rangers finally come to life and knock Andujar out when they score six times in the bottom half of the inning and tie the score at 8-8. Each team adds another run in their half of the eighth to knot the score at nine going into the ninth. Then the Sox score twice in the ninth inning and shut down the Rangers for a 11-9 win.

The crowd on hand tonight totals 46,481, and the game takes over three and one half hours to play. The Texas fans, while wildly enthusiastic and extremely well behaved, seemed to cheer and boo in a less than knowledgeable fashion about the game. Never mind, they had a great time even though their team lost. Getting out of the ballpark is a mess and Marc and I walk the mile back to our motel rather than deal with the long lines waiting for public transportation. It's a clean, well put together stadium but the congestion getting in and out is a definite problem and the only major minus for Arlington. Tomorrow we'll be getting an early start for Houston and an afternoon game with my San Francisco Giants.

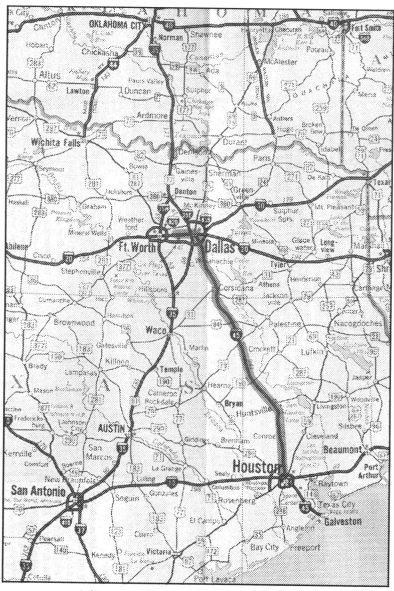

Arlington to Houston via I-20 and I-45.

CHAPTER VI

Houston—The Astro Dome

We leave Arlington at 7:00 AM as we have to travel almost 300 miles and get to Houston for a 1:30 game with the Giants. We were surprised at the beauty of the scenery between Dallas and Houston. There are soft rolling hills with lots of greenery and large leafy trees. Texas, like California, is a state that covers vast amount of miles: 850 from west to east and 950 north to south.

The Astros were one of the first National League expansion teams. They entered the league in 1962 along with the New York Mets. The Houston franchise won two Western Division titles, one in 1980 and the other in 1986, but they have yet to win the National League pennant. Known as the Colt 45's before being renamed the Astros in 1965, they play their home games in the Astro Dome, the very first of its kind—a domed stadium. It is referred to as the "eighth wonder of the world" and set the precedent for the next four which were built in Seattle, Montreal, Minnesota and Toronto.

Why domed? Was baseball meant to be played in covered symmetrical stadiums with artificial grass? Houston's dome was built for protection against the heat and humidity of southern Texas and the others to keep fans warm and dry from the cold and rain of more northern climates. The jury is still out on domed stadiums, at least as far as this fan is concerned. Yes, they work for the purposes I previously stated, but being in a domed stadium makes for a kind of claustrophobia and gives me some discomfort. It's a closed feeling and I need to state here that this is a very personal observation and may not be shared by a lot of fans. The artificial turf doesn't help any either.

I dearly miss the old stadiums that were built right in the neighborhoods, where people could stand on their roofs to watch the game. There was real grass, the kind that only God makes, with smells and stains. Real stadiums had marvelous nooks and corners where balls ricocheted away from pursuing fielders.

Baseball wasn't meant to be played in thermostatically controlled, artificially sanitized environments, with controls to keep you cool, warm, happy, comfortable. Baseball was meant to be endured by defying all the elements that nature could throw at us. We sweat, we froze, we got rained on and we knew we were having one of life's great experiences! The umpires had to work a lot harder than they do today. Almost every playing field had its own unique layout, each one requiring a different set of ground rules, often to be redone each time a new game was played. Stadiums didn't come stamped out of a cookie cutter in user friendly formats as they did in the 60's and 70's. Today, I am glad they are getting back to the old style stadiums as evidenced by The Ballpark at Arlington, Jacobs Field in Cleveland, Oriole Park at Camden Yards in Baltimore and Coors Field in Denver.

After my recovery from mononucleosis, another interest came along—
touch football. It was great fun playing in our narrow streets lined with
cars. Oh yes, it was the same streets, same cars, same Bronx. Years later,
when I read about the Kennedys' having such fun on the vast fields and
beaches of their family compound in Hyannisport, I thought then as I do
now, that they couldn't possibly be as happy as we were when we played
among the parked cars of the Bronx, NYC!

The play was down the street and cut behind the maroon car and I'll hit
you with the pass. My relatively small stature enabled me to be as nimble
as a water bug. That, combined with my endless hours of practicing, made
me a formidable player.

We arrive in Houston in plenty of time for the game and check
into our motel. It is hot and sticky and we are grateful that we will
be watching baseball under the climate controlled dome. Say what
I will about the good old days of real baseball, there's no denying
that on a day like today in Houston, some air conditioning will feel
mighty good.

My Giants are in the depths of a real swoon which started in June
and shows no sign of abating. The Astros knock out San Francisco
starter Osvaldo Fernandez in the second inning by scoring four
runs. The Astros lead is 5-2 going into the seventh when they replace
their starter Mike Hampton. The Giants rally in the late innings due
to several mishaps by Houston fielders. In the top of the ninth, the
Giants trail 7-6 with one out and the bases loaded, and Barry Bonds
and Matt Williams coming to bat. However, Astro reliever Billy
Wagner is able to strike out both Bonds and Williams and the game
is over.

This completes almost 20% of the Challenge. I've seen six games
and driven about 2,500 miles. Our next game will be in Miami on
August 8th which gives us four days of travel.

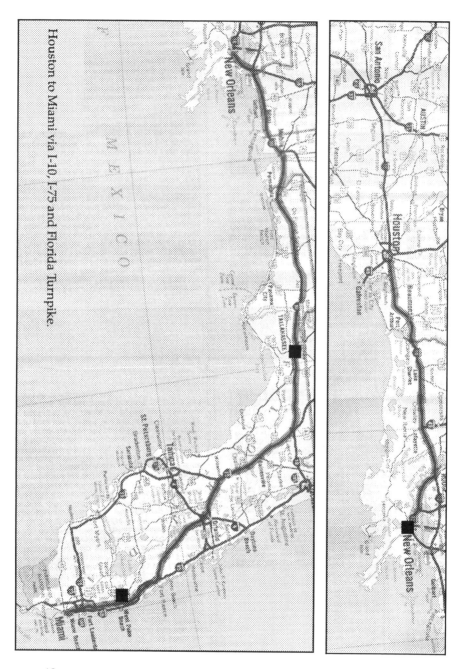

Houston to Miami via I-10, I-75 and Florida Turnpike.

CHAPTER VII

Miami—Pro Players Park

From Houston it's about 1,200 miles to Miami and our next game on August 8th.

We have four days to get there, so we intend to take in some of the more interesting sites along the way. With that in mind we plan to make New Orleans our next stop.

It's almost noon and we're heading out of Houston. The day is hot and muggy, temperatures already in the high 90's. We finally leave Texas, after covering just shy of 1,000 miles, as we cross into Louisiana. Interstate 10, which travels through the southern tier of Louisiana, passes some gorgeous scenery. I-10 looks more like a parkway than it does your usual interstate. Smooth roadways along with heavily wooded trees and green grass are very prevalent. This area reminds me somewhat of the Palisades Interstate Parkway in New Jersey, albeit without the cliffs. We pass over the Lake Charles River and see billboards for riverboats and casinos. The odometer reads 3,360 miles and we are really in bayou country, going over pontoon type bridges built out of the swamps on huge pylons. At 4:30 in the afternoon we cross the mighty Mississippi and see the state capitol of Baton Rouge. We don't stop, as we want to have lots of time to spend in the exciting city of New Orleans.

We pull into New Orleans late in the afternoon and check into our motel which is just a few blocks from the French Quarter. We populate Pat O'Brien's watering hole and listen to jazz at Preservation Hall. We even spend a little time on a Mississippi riverboat playing blackjack and feeling very much part of the "New Orleans experience".

We leave the next morning for Tallahassee and I reflect on what we have just experienced. New Orleans is a very cosmopolitan city but I admit to having some discomfort while there. There's a decadent quality, sex acts almost advertised on street corners, services freely available that I couldn't put on our web site or want to.

We are driving through a very tiny portion of Mississippi and Alabama along the Gulf of Mexico. The landscape is very similar to that of Louisiana. The whole southern tier encompassing these three states on I-10 is really a treat to drive. Lush and green, it is a picture postcard of the deep South. It's coming up on noon and we're about an hour from Pensacola where we plan to stop and take in the Naval Air Museum. We pass through Mobile, Alabama and go through a tunnel. We emerge into a beautiful scene of huge trees and clusters of brightly colored flowers. Then it's across Mobile Bay on a pontoon bridge called Jubilee Parkway. At 2 PM we cross into Florida's panhandle and arrive at Pensacola and the museum. After viewing the show at the I-Max Theater, which is a treat and puts us right into the history of flight, we are on our way again. We will be losing another hour very soon and be on eastern daylight time. We cross over the Chattahoochee Bridge made famous in song and folklore and we're now in the eastern time zone when we arrive in Tallahassee and complete our trip for this day.

The next morning we are up early and drive non-stop for six hours to my parent's home in Lake Worth, Florida. I will make this my home base for the next few days. I plan to do laundry, catch up on my mail and spend some quality time with my parents. Marc will go back to work for the next two days and we will hook up on Friday night when we'll start the next leg.

Tomorrow evening, Thursday, August 8th, both my mother and dad will accompany me to the Florida Marlins game in Miami. The Marlins will be hosting the New York Mets. This will create a difficult problem for my father, as he has long loved the Mets. Being from New York, they were his team from the time the franchise came to be. Now that he lives in Florida, there is mixed emotion and it promises to be exciting just watching his reactions. Of course, knowing the history of these two teams, the real suspense will be to see which one of them will find a new and unique way to lose! My dad tells me he will wear a Mets cap and root for the Marlins. Either way one of his teams can't lose, unless you believe in a 23 inning tie game!

The Florida Marlins are one of the newest National League franchises, entering the league in 1993 along with the Colorado Rockies. These two teams brought the National League to its present size of 14 teams and finally in line with the 14 teams the American League has had since 1977. This expansion also brought about a realignment in both leagues and the formation of three divisions in each league, which will be discussed later in greater detail.

Being a NY Giants fan, I spent much time at the Polo Grounds. There was no other major league outfield like it. The left and right field foul lines ended at short porches for balls hit down the lines. Center field was made for Willie (that is Mays if you didn't know). The "say hey kid" could roam and cover any inept left and/or right fielder. You could count on one hand the number of balls hit into the center field bleachers, as it was approximately 450 feet from home plate. I remember Dee Fondy of the Chicago Cubs hitting a ball to the deepest part of center field and it bouncing off of the clubhouse steps.

I miss the old places like New York's Polo Grounds, Brooklyn's Ebbets Field, Pittsburgh's Forbes Field, Cincinnati's Crosley Field, and St. Louis' Sportsman's Park. We still have a few of them left—Tiger stadium in Detroit, Fenway Park in Boston and the famous Wrigley Field in Chicago.

Radio was a great vehicle to keep us deeply enthralled with the game. The announcers would create an atmosphere of suspense that left us fascinated. The likes of Mel Allen, Red Barber, Russ Hodges, Ernie Harwell, Bob Prince and Vince Scully would create wonderfully vivid pictures inside our heads and hearts that no television screen of today could ever compete with. The ball getting lost in the ivy of Wrigley Field or landing on Bedford Avenue in Brooklyn: this was what baseball was all about. The Green Monster in Fenway, the terrace at Crosley Field, the caverns at Forbes Field: these, and the voices of the men who, day by day, season after season, brought baseball to us, were our only truth.

It's now Thursday, August 8th, day 14 of the MLBC and my parents and I are driving to Miami for tonight's Mets/Marlins game. Automobile access to and from the ballpark is the best in the majors. They have dedicated entrance and exit ramps leading to and from the Florida Turnpike.

The Marlins play their home games in Miami's Pro Players Park, formerly known as Joe Robbie Stadium. This stadium, octagonal in shape, was built for the Miami Dolphins football team. This is a very clean stadium, double decked all around, but done in somewhat garish colors of orange and teal green. It seems to me that this color combination belongs in a circus, not a baseball stadium. It has two levels of seating with luxury boxes in between. There is a huge scoreboard which makes up the entire left field wall. Along the right side of the outfield there are field level seats.

The starting pitchers are Pete Harnish for the Mets and Kevin Brown (the National Leagues ERA leader) for the Marlins. We are treated to a sensational pitcher's duel as both men are really on their game. The game is scoreless through seven innings. In the Mets half of the eighth, with one out, Brown walks the next batter. Bernard "innocent until proven" Guilkey then takes a Kevin Brown fastball and parks it for a two run homer. Todd Hundley immediately follows Guilkey with a back-to-back solo blast that sends Brown to the showers and gives the Mets a 3-0 lead which turns out to be the final score. So much for a tie!

This concludes leg two of the journey and a total of seven ball games. It's now back to my folks' house for the night. On our way back the odometer indicates that I've completed 4,000 miles of the MLBC. Tomorrow, Friday, is a day off and my last chance to spend time with my parents for quite awhile. I'll also pick up Marc and on Saturday morning we'll begin the trek north and our next stop, Atlanta.

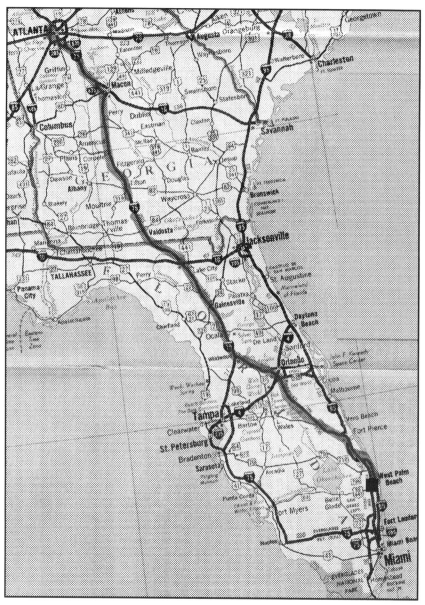

Lake Worth to Atlanta via Florida Turnpike and I-75.

CHAPTER VIII

Atlanta—Fulton County Stadium

We leave Lake Worth early in the morning as we begin leg three of the MLBC. It's Saturday, August 10th, and the game between the Colorado Rockies and the Atlanta Braves will be played on Sunday evening. Our original plan was to take two days to get to Atlanta and stop overnight in southern Georgia. However, Marc convinces me that it should be no problem to do the 600 mile drive in just one day. This would also give us some sightseeing time at the venues of the Olympic Games which had ended barely two weeks before.

The first part of the trip is traveled over the same road we had come south on just a few days before, from Tallahassee to Lake Worth on the Sunshine State Parkway. We make very good time and by 11 AM we have crossed into Georgia on I-75. The roads are excellent, the best we've seen so far. It's apparent that the State of

Georgia has done some serious repairing and upgrading of facilities for visitors to the Olympics. Thickly wooded pines on both sides of the road add to the beauty of the highway and make this part of the drive a thoroughly enjoyable experience. Another perk of this area is the price of gasoline. They are the lowest in the country at just about a dollar a gallon. We learn that a major pipeline for gas distribution goes through Atlanta.

We get to Atlanta in just about nine hours and check into our motel in Marietta, which is about twenty miles north of the city. We take a quick trip to the Olympic site but don't get out of the car as the entire area has been turned into a kind of street market with hundreds (or so it seems) of booths of one kind or another selling food, memorabilia, etc. It's terribly crowded and the traffic discourages us from stopping. We head back to Marietta where we have dinner in a local Italian restaurant and then off to an amusement center for some fun and games before we call it a night.

The Braves franchise, which was one of the original 16, began in 1876, in Boston, where they played until 1952. They then relocated to Milwaukee where they spent 13 years from 1953 through 1965. They won two National League pennants there in 1957 and 58, and one World Series in 1957. I vividly recall the 1957 World Series against the New York Yankees. It was the third game of the series and the first time a World Series game was played in Milwaukee. Tony Kubek of the Yankees hit a home run in County Stadium and you could literally hear a pin drop. I've never to this day witnessed a ballpark being that silent after a home run. Some moments never leave you and that was one of them.

In 1966, they moved to Atlanta and have been there ever since. For many years in the late 70's and 80's the Braves were the doormat of the National League. As cycles turn around they have been arguably the best team in baseball for the last five years. Although they have a very good team in all aspects of the game, their standout strength is in their pitching staff, without question the best in baseball. This franchise has won numerous pennants and three World Series titles, one in each location.

I turned fourteen in 1956 which proved to be a very interesting time in my life. First, my family moved to the other side of town, the Pelham Parkway section in the northeast corner of the Bronx. The new area was significantly different from the old neighborhood. No apartment buildings and not too many kids. The streets were not designed for stickball—too many hills and no sewers to use as base markers. I would be attending Christopher Columbus High School instead of the rough and tough James Monroe in my old neighborhood. We lived in one half of a two family home nowadays called a duplex.

In June I was shipped off to southeast Florida to spend the summer with my grandparents. Going to Florida was a new experience for me. I had never traveled that far from home before and was the first in my family to fly. I'll always remember that flight. It was on an Eastern Airlines Constellation, at night, with two intermediate stops, over six hours and very scary.

In Florida I was picked to play sandlot baseball for the Boutwell Dairy team. I pitched and played second base when I wasn't pitching. I made the all star team and was the winning pitcher and MVP. I was asked to come back the following year, but that didn't pan out. I also took tennis lessons that summer, but tennis was not my cup of tea.

In the fall, my Aunt Belle took me to see my first ever World Series game. It was at Yankee Stadium where the New York Yankees hosted the Brooklyn Dodgers. My aunt got expensive tickets, box seats right behind third base. What a treat! I got dressed in my Yankee uniform for that occasion, with number 10 (shortstop Phil Rizzuto's number) on my back. The Theriot Avenue Boys decided to have the same uniform as that of the Yankees, and much against my deepest feelings, I had to get one to be part of the team.

It's Sunday morning and a problem seems to be developing in my left leg. I noticed some redness and tenderness when we were in New Orleans but didn't give it a second thought. While in Florida it caught my attention again, but I wasn't too concerned. Now it is a size similar to half of a golf ball and I feel the need to have it checked out. Marc and I head for an urgent care center a few miles from the motel. The doctor says I have developed cellulitis, which is an inflammation of the soft tissue, and prescribes a fairly strong antibiotic.

After filling my prescription, Marc and I take in some of the sites in the area. We drive through some beautiful residential sections. The area reminds me of the place I lived in New York State, heavily wooded, lush and green. We call on a couple of friends I know living in the Atlanta area, but unfortunately they are not at home. We get back to the motel at 4 PM. After relaxing for awhile we leave for dinner at the famous Varsity restaurant and then to the baseball game.

The Braves play their home games at Fulton County Stadium, known as "The Launching Pad", since fly balls seem to leave the playing field in a hurry. It is among the crop of stadiums built in the 60's and 70's as a dual purpose stadium for both football and baseball. These type of stadiums are circular by design and completely closed. Most of these fields had or still have artificial grass. In Atlanta they currently have the real stuff. For next season (1997) the Braves will move across the street to Ted Turner Stadium (the Olympic Stadium) which is currently undergoing a reconfiguration for baseball.

Today's game between the Colorado Rockies and Atlanta Braves will be an unusual Sunday night game as it will be on national television. The game is delayed one hour and ten minutes due to thunderstorms. When it finally gets under way Roger Bailey of the Rockies opposes John Smoltz of the Braves.

Colorado scores first on an Ellis Burks' solo homer in the fourth. Bailey, who pitches superbly, is lifted for a pinch hitter in the top of the eighth. He pitches seven scoreless innings while allowing just three base hits. Marvin Freeman comes in for Colorado to pitch the bottom of the eighth and gives up four runs on three hits, a walk and a hit batsman. This is another instance where a manager removes a starting pitcher who is in total control for a reliever who is ineffective. Smoltz, who has pitched eight strong innings and records ten strikeouts gives way to the Braves closer Mark Wohlers who retires the Rockies in the ninth. The final score is Atlanta 4, Rockies 1 before a crowd of 32,961.

After the game Marc and I drive back to our motel in Marietta, Georgia and call it a night.

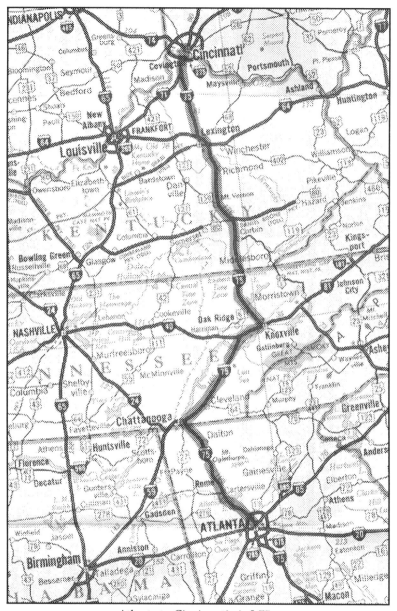

Atlanta to Cincinnati via I-75.

CHAPTER IX

Cincinnati—Riverfront Stadium

Today is Monday, August 12th, and we have a long day's drive ahead of us—approximately 460 miles north on Interstate 75 to the Queen's City, Cincinnati. My leg seems to be getting more swollen. I have the chills and feel I have fever. Marc has taken over the driving for the day as I doze off and on.

Although it is raining most of the way, the northwest corner of Georgia and eastern Tennessee is just beautiful. We travel through the Smoky Mountains with its lush green rolling terrain. After leaving Tennessee, Interstate 75 goes due north right through central Kentucky. Passing by Lexington we get into horse country. The finest thoroughbreds and standardbreds are raised in this part of the country. We arrive at our hotel in Covington, Kentucky at 4 PM after seven and one half hours on the road. Covington is situated on the south bank of the Ohio River just across from Cincinnati and Riverfront Stadium. Our hotel is circular and we have a magnificent view of the river, stadium and the city from our window.

The Cincinnati franchise began way back in 1869 and were called the Red Stockings. In 1912, they moved into Crosley Field and were known as the Redlegs. Crosley Field was the site of MLB's first night game in 1935. They played in that ballpark for 57 years before moving into Riverfront Stadium in 1970. Somewhere in that period the name was shortened to the Reds.

Riverfront Stadium is another one of those multipurpose stadiums built in the 60's and 70's. The main difference between this place and Atlanta's Fulton County Stadium is that Riverfront has artificial grass. Otherwise it is closed and circular in design.

Riverfront was the home of "The Big Red Machine" in the 70's. The likes of Pete Rose, Johnny Bench, Tony Perez and Joe Morgan provided one the most potent offensives in modern day baseball. They were the team of the 70's, winning four pennants and two world championships. Their last World Series victory occurred in 1990 when they defeated the Oakland Athletics. Overall they have won nine pennants and five World Series titles.

My new school yard gave me a different kind of "playing field": it was concrete. We played softball on this field. It had a short left field with a handball court bisecting it. Center field had a garden to work around, but right field was wide open and quite expansive. My father played softball with us kids every now and then. I remember him hitting a ball over the left field fence and right through the bedroom window of the adjacent house. It was a ground rule double, a broken window and the end of that game, as we all took off.

The school yard also had good fast pitching-in areas with the handball wall and school chimney becoming excellent backstops. This is where I really developed my pitching techniques. My fast ball, curve and drop were getting pretty good. But the pitch that separated me from the pack was my "jiggler". It was thrown like a screwball and acted like a "knuckler". It would dance as it reached the batter and then move abruptly in an erratic unpredictable direction.

I was always throwing my arm out and had to resort to playing basketball until my arm felt good enough to get back to pitching. I would go to the school yard around 8:00 on Saturday morning before most of my friends were awake and practice shooting with my "off" hand, that is my left. Being one of the smallest kids, at 5'2" and 100 pounds soaking wet, I was a "leaper". They called me the white boy with black blood. I was very proud when black and white kids said that. Remember, this was mid 1950's America and we didn't know from politically savvy speech. It was considered the greatest compliment to be told you played as well as a black. Of course, in those days, they were called Negroes and life along those lines was a whole lot simpler. Not fair or even right, mind you, but simpler.

The basketball courts we played on were very different from today's arenas. Ours had concrete floors with a flush steel pole supporting the backboard and hoop. This created a much more dangerous situation than today's wooden floors and recessed supports. We were always being injured, but bruised and bloodied we played on, "Bronx Style"!

We take a shuttle bus from our hotel across the river to the ballpark. What a great way to go. The weather is just perfect, 72 degrees and low humidity. These are the best conditions that we've had thus far. The Reds are hosting the Dodgers and send John Smiley to the mound to oppose Ramon Martinez.

Mike Piazzi gets things going early with a first inning solo home run. The Dodgers add two more runs in the fourth while the Reds get on the board in the fifth with a run of their own and the score stands at 3-1 after five. In the Dodger sixth Eric Karros hits a fly ball to deep center field. Thomas Howard, the Reds center fielder leaps at the wall and the ball glances off his glove and rolls on the top of the wall for about ten feet before falling to the playing field. This is the first time I have ever seen this happen, live or on television. Anyhow, it is ruled a ground rule double. The Dodgers score three times in the inning, extending their lead to 6-1, and knock John Smiley out of the game. The Reds get their second run on a Thomas

Howard homer in the seventh and now trail 6-2. The Reds rally in the bottom of the ninth off Dodger relievers, Osuna and Worrel. In fact, they score three runs and have the tying and go ahead runs aboard with two outs and Kevin Mitchell at bat. Worrel gets Mitchell to ground out and he preserves the 6-5 victory.

After the game Marc and I take the shuttle bus back to the hotel. Tomorrow is a travel day as we head for the "windy city".

Cincinnati to Chicago via I-74, I-65 and I-90.

CHAPTER X

Chicago—Comiskey Park

Day 19, Tuesday, August 13th, is a travel day from Cincinnati to Chicago. Today's drive takes us through Ohio and the farmlands of Indiana. The last fifty miles of this 300 mile segment puts us into the heaviest commercial trucking corridor in the nation. Interstate 80 & 90 which runs below the southern tip of Lake Michigan, at Gary, Indiana, accommodates more "18 wheelers" than it does automobiles. Also contributing to the congestion is the fact that it's the hub for several other major interstates which distributes traffic to all other parts of the country.

We arrive in "Chicagoland" at around 3 PM. We'll be staying north of the city in Glenview. We'll make this our home base for the next five days and four ball games.

My leg has not responded to the antibiotic and the condition appears to be getting worse. We decide to go to the emergency room at a Chicago hospital. There the doctors believe that the lump is abscessed and they decide to stick a syringe in it to allow it to drain. After penetrating the lump they find no infection so they close the wound, prescribe a stronger antibiotic and suggest I come back in two days to have it looked at again.

Up until 1991 the White Sox played at old Comiskey Park which is on the south end of Chicago. That old ballpark was constructed in 1910 and lasted some 80 years before it was torn down. My mother, who grew up in Chicago, remembers her mother taking her on the streetcar to see the White Sox play at Comiskey.

The White Sox now play at the new Comiskey Park, just across the street from the old Comiskey. This new ballpark, unlike the ones now being built, is not designed to look old. There isn't a bad seat in the house as there are no pillars to obstruct your view. There is an extra wide concourse that circles the stadium and contains food stands, amusements, souvenirs and sports memorabilia. You can walk around the concourse and keep an eye on the ball game at all times. The bleacher seats, where we are sitting, have individual backs and are quite comfortable.

This franchise won five American League pennants and two World Series since their inception in 1901. The last pennant was in 1959, when they were dubbed the "Go Sox". This name was given to them in response to their style of play. The '59 "Go Sox" had a superb defensive team with great pitching and lots of speed. They had won many games that season by scores of 1-0 and 2-1. They would score runs without a base hit; a walk, stolen base, and two sacrifice outs were common. Their last World Series title was way back in 1917, which is the longest dry spell of any of the original American League franchises.

It was 1957, the year that the Giants and Dodgers announced that they were leaving New York. I was fifteen years old and I thought I would die from the pain of it! How could my idols, my heroes, my reason for living do this to me? However, I still had radio. I would religiously listen to Les Keiter, a sportscaster of that day, recreate the San Francisco Giants' games. He would read the tape of the game in a studio with piped-in crowd noise, a stick and a wooden block to replicate the games at Seal Stadium where the Giants now played. Of course, TV was in its infancy and televising live games that were not local was a long ways away. What did we know? We thrilled at the sounds and feel of the game recreated in a studio. Our mind's eyes were more vivid than any camera could ever be.

Seal Stadium was located in the Potrero district of San Francisco, just ten miles from the Pacific Ocean. It was situated in an area of the city which has the most desirable climate. However, the fog came in quite regularly and Les would describe fans wearing winter clothing, huddled over paper cups of hot bouillon. This was quite a change for me. Imagine a baseball game with overcoats and hot soup in the middle of summer! Today's Giants play in an even colder and very windy stadium called Candlestick Park (3-Com Park) right smack on San Francisco Bay. 3-Com Park became the official name a few months ago, but for most diehard San Franciscans, fans or not, it is now and will always be "The Stick".

In the 1950's, several changes occurred within the MLB franchises. The Boston Braves moved to Milwaukee in 1953. The St. Louis Browns relocated and became the Baltimore Orioles in 1954. In 1955, the Philadelphia Athletics moved to Kansas City. And the Giants and Dodgers left New York in 1958 for San Francisco and Los Angeles respectively. The structure of the two leagues hadn't changed nor did the 154 game schedule. As of 1960 the MLB teams were aligned as follows:

National League	American League
Chicago Cubs	Baltimore Orioles
Cincinnati Redlegs	Boston Red Sox
Los Angeles Dodgers	Chicago White Sox
Milwaukee Braves	Cleveland Indians

Philadelphia Phillies	Detroit Tigers
Pittsburgh Pirates	Kansas City Athletics
St. Louis Cardinals	New York Yankees
San Francisco Giants	Washington Senators

We leave our motel Wednesday morning around eleven o'clock for a day game at Comiskey. We leave a bit early as we need to drive from the north end of Chicago to the southern part of the city and don't know how long it will take. The White Sox are hosting the Eastern Division leaders, the New York Yankees. Jim Baldwin is given the start for the Sox and will oppose the Yankees ace Andy Pettitte. The game is scoreless for five and one half innings. In the bottom half of the sixth, Frank "the big hurt" Thomas gets things going with a solo homer into the center field bleachers and gives the Sox a 1-0 lead. The Yankees come right back in their half of the seventh with two runs, including a Tito Martinez home run, and take a 2-1 lead. The Yankees add another run in the eighth on a Derek Jeter solo blast. That is all that is needed as Mariano Rivera comes in to relieve Pettitte and pitches scoreless eighth and ninth innings.

Tomorrow, the 15th, is an off day and Marc and I will take in some of the sights of Chicago. Our next game will be in Minneapolis on the 16th.

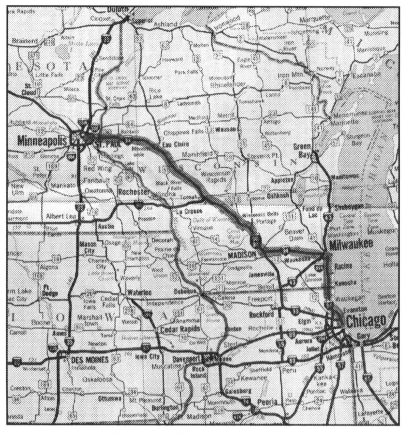

Chicago to Minneapolis via I-94.

CHAPTER XI

Minneapolis—Metrodome

Thursday, August 15th, and day 21 of the MLBC. We pass the 6,000 mile mark of my dream trip today and it is time to take the car in for an oil change. So far no complaints on the Dodge Intrepid. It rides like a big sedan which is good for this long trip. However, I do prefer the smaller better handling sport sedans for my everyday driving pleasure.

Marc and I spend the day driving around Chicago. We go to the Old Orchard outdoor shopping mall with stores of the likes of Bloomingdales, Nordstroms, Lord and Taylor and Saks Fifth Avenue, just to name a few of the more pricey establishments. The weather is just great, high 70's and low humidity. We also go to the hospital to have my leg checked. The doctor feels that the swelling and redness are subsiding as the antibiotic is taking over.

We have an early dinner at Michael Jordan's restaurant, a real fun place to spend a few hours. After dinner we drive up Lake Shore Drive, passing Soldier Field, Buckingham Fountain, Navy Pier and the shores of Lake Michigan. We witness swimmers, joggers, roller bladers, beach volley ball, softball games, et al. Taking Sheridan Road we drive by the gorgeous estates and through the beautiful campus of Northwestern University. Great sights! By the way, regular unleaded gasoline prices are up to $1.30 per gallon, a far cry from the $1.00 per gallon in Georgia.

On Friday morning we head north to Minneapolis and the Hubert H. Humphrey Metrodome, known as the giant hefty bag. Our 400 mile drive takes us through the agricultural farms in southeastern Wisconsin. These give way to dairy farms as we head west towards the Minnesota border. The scenery is quite beautiful as everything is green and in full bloom. I know that for a fact, because my grass and pollen allergies are absolutely at their worst.

Before reaching Minneapolis we stop off at Eau Claire, Wisconsin, seventy-five miles to the east, and check into our motel. This will give us a little over an hour head start tomorrow as we have a day game at Wrigley Field in Chicago. We also have time to visit with a friend and client of mine in Brooklyn Park, a suburb of Minneapolis. Fortunately he and his wife and all of their nine children are at home this weekend. After leaving their home we proceed to downtown Minneapolis and have a light dinner at Hubert's, a famous landmark across the street from the Metrodome.

In my mid teens I joined the 92nd Street YMHA in Manhattan, otherwise known as the Jewish YMCA. Here I began a new interest, bowling. No automatic pinsetters in those days, just me and Jimmy Katz setting them up for each other. We learned billiards and pool, played pickup basketball; oh yes, the Y was a wonderful place for a city kid. Everything was under one roof, except of course my beloved baseball. But I would always go back to "The Game".

The Metrodome is the second of five domed stadiums we will see. It is quite a bit newer and nicer looking inside than the Astro Dome. The color scheme of blue seats, dark walls and gray/white ceiling is more appealing than the Houston dome. Also, it is easier to follow the flight of a pop fly due to the opaque ceiling. It has two levels of seating with luxury boxes in between. We sit directly behind home plate and 29 rows up, great seats!

This franchise actually began in 1901 as the Washington (DC) Senators. They became the Minnesota Twins in 1961 and played in Bloomington until 1981. In 1982, they relocated to Minneapolis and the Metrodome. The franchise has won six American League pennants, three in each city. In Washington, the Senators won one World Series while the Twins have two to their credit.

For tonight's game the Twins are hosting the Toronto Blue Jays. Juan Guzman will start for the Blue Jays and oppose Brad Radke of the Twins. The Blue Jays score single runs in the second, third and fifth, while the Twins get single runs in the fourth and fifth, and the score stands at 3-2 favor of the Blue Jays. In the home half of the seventh, Marty Cordova hits a two run homer to give the Twins a 4-3 lead. In the top of the ninth, pinch hitter John Olerud's double scores the tying run which eventually sends the game into extra innings. In the bottom of the tenth, Minnesota first baseman Stahoviak (who is having a great game in the field, at the plate and on the bases) stretches a routine base hit into a double. With Dave Hollins at bat and a 3-0 count, he is given the green light. He takes full advantage of the situation by driving a ball off of the giant "hefty bag" in right field to score the winning run for a Twins' 5-4 ten inning victory. Although the game lasted three hours and twenty-five minutes which could have been mind numbing, it kept the fans' attention and was very exciting.

After the game we drive back to Eau Claire to spend the night.

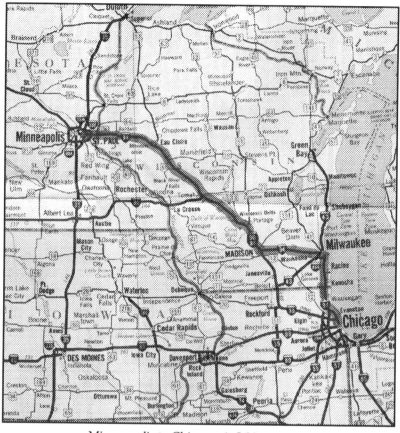

Minneapolis to Chicago via I-94.

CHAPTER XII

Chicago—Wrigley Field

Going to Chicago and Wrigley Field from Minneapolis was not my original plan. This change in schedule was due to Marc's ability to obtain corporate tickets for the Cubs game on Saturday. To this end, I swapped Chicago for Milwaukee. Although this caused an additional 200 miles, it seemed well worth it, as getting Cubs' tickets for a weekend game is quite difficult.

We follow our tracks back to Chicago and have enough time to check back into our motel in Glenview. We drive to the north end of Chicago and take the elevated (EL) train to the "friendly confines" of Wrigley Field. It's like I stepped back in time fifty years to when I lived in the Bronx. The "EL" goes past apartment buildings, neighborhood stores, and every ethnic community. We arrive at the Addison Avenue station and exit onto the crowded streets that surround Wrigley. The ballpark is situated right in the heart of a residential area. It was constructed in 1914 when it was known as Weeghman Park. Wrigley Field was the last major league stadium to add lights. That addition occurred in 1988 with much controversy.

It is a madhouse, with music in the streets and places to eat, drink, party and purchase paraphernalia. You can get any type of food in any type of environment. From bagels to zucchini, "the streets" have it all. Then into the friendly confines, through the tunnel and you suddenly fall into the nostalgia of this place. The first thing I notice is the brick wall that surrounds a good portion of the field, then the ivy covering the outfield wall, and the thick, real grass on the field surface. As I gaze upward I see the famous left field bleachers and the roof tops of the houses beyond the outfield. There are stands constructed on these roof tops filled with onlookers, barbecues smoking away, along with beer and other spirits aplenty. There is a party going on all over this place and you can't help getting caught up in it. Harry Carey is in his usual place in the booth, the massive old organ is blaring out the wonderful music and I say to myself, there is nothing like Wrigley, nothing!

Looking back at the field, I notice the manually operated scoreboard, and the lack of any advertising within the confines. This has them all beat by miles and you don't even have to like baseball to enjoy it. Win, lose or draw, the fans love their "Cubbies" and this place. To illustrate this, almost every seat in the ballpark continually sells out even though the Cubs have had the longest dry spell of any other franchise, providing their loyal fans with neither a pennant or world championship. It's been over 50 years since they won the National League crown and almost 90 years since they delivered a world championship to their followers. Although they haven't had a winning year of late, they do have 16 pennants and two world championships to their credit.

In high school I competed in three intramural sports: baseball, basketball and flag football. I finally had started growing—five inches in my last year of High School—and I was now all of 5'7" and a whopping 118 pounds.

After graduating Columbus High I attended Bronx Community College. I really hated school and just wanted to do what I did best, play sports. While in college I was on two teams, bowling and basketball. The college, unfortunately, did not have a baseball team. I carried a 205 bowling average which I was very proud of as the top pros in those days averaged 212.

Oh, by the way, there is also a game being played today on this beautiful afternoon for baseball at Wrigley. It is standing room only as the Cubs beat the Houston Astros handily by the score of 12-3. Steve Trachsel pitches a complete game (very rare these days) and doesn't allow an earned run. And as is the tradition here, Harry Carey leads the fans through "take me out to the ball game" during the seventh inning stretch. This was an experience I will never forget.

Chicago to Milwaukee via I-94.

CHAPTER XIII

Milwaukee—County Stadium

It's Sunday morning, August 18th, and I'm driving to Chicago's O'Hare airport. Marc will be leaving me and the MLBC as he is flying back home to Florida. I will really miss his company. We had some great times together on this journey. We saw a great deal of this vast country together and experienced some beautiful scenery. He was a enormous help as he did the majority of the driving when we were together and was a good companion.

After dropping Marc off, I have to "high tail" it to Milwaukee for a day game. It's about a ninety mile drive to County Stadium in Milwaukee. This route is "old hat" by now as Marc and I had been on it from Chicago to Minneapolis and back again. The city is in the midst of its Italian festival and huge crowds are expected throughout the metropolitan area.

Milwaukee has had major league baseball on a nonsequential basis for almost 100 years. It was the home of an American League franchise for one year in 1901, and then the home of the Braves franchise for 13 years, from 1953 through 1965. Since 1970 the Brewers have made Milwaukee their home. This latest franchise came from Seattle, where they were known as the Pilots for one year in 1969. The Brewers have won one American League title back in 1982. They lost their only World Series opportunity that year to the St. Louis Cardinals.

Milwaukee's County Stadium was built in 1952 for the Milwaukee Braves. You find the best tailgate parties in the parking lots that surround the stadium. The smoke from the barbecues can be seen during the game as the coals cool down. Inside this stadium you find the best bratwurst in the majors. Speaking about the stadium, it is old, but not like Wrigley's old. It's a double decked stadium with sky boxes in between. The entire outfield has bleacher type seating. There is a huge scoreboard in right center field. There is also a giant-sized beer keg and beer mug foaming over in center field, the stadiums' signature.

In basketball I was an average player due to my size which is a decided detriment playing that game. So I concentrated on my skills at bowling. I used to test myself with several stops on the pro bowlers tour. I was bowling with the likes of Ernie Schlegel, Mike Limengello and Dewey Blair, to name a few.

I drove my parents crazy in the late 50's and early 60's. I was still living at home, hanging around race tracks and bowling alleys into the wee hours of the morning. They certainly did not approve of the characters with whom I associated—Two Finger Izzy, Pepe LaRue and Big John the Chinaman to name a few. These guys would bet on anything and everything both inside and outside the alleys.

I worked part time in order to feed my gambling habit. I would be at Yonkers or Roosevelt raceways about two to three times a week. On the

weekends after taking my Saturday night date home I would wind up in the
bowling alleys until 6 AM. I didn't have much time for baseball.

Today's game pits the Brewers against their geographically close rivals, the Chicago White Sox. Many White Sox fans make their way up to Milwaukee for the series between these two teams. The game has lots of excitement throughout. Every time the Brewers take the lead the Sox battle back to close within one run or tie the game. The Brewers push across the go ahead run in the bottom of the eighth which they make stand up for the game winner. The final score is Brewers 8 and the White Sox 7, before a very vocal packed house of 33,094.

Well, this concludes the third leg of the MLBC. I have now traveled 7,000 miles in 24 days and witnessed 13 ball games. I'll now leave Milwaukee and drive about 200 miles around Lake Michigan to Benton Harbor, Michigan where I'll spend the night. Benton Harbor is located on the eastern shore of Lake Michigan just across from Evanston, Illinois.

I travel back across the Illinois-Wisconsin border for the fourth time in three days. Then I'm again on the Tristate Tollway which I have lived on for the past six days. This roadway runs through the northeastern corner of Illinois around Chicago and Lake Michigan and connects Illinois with Wisconsin and Indiana. This Tristate Tollway is the busiest interstate hub in the US, connecting more interstate highways to the Chicago area than you can imagine. Besides its major spur routes of I-294, I-290 and I-190 you find I-94 heading north into Milwaukee, I-90 northwest to Minneapolis, I-88 going west to Iowa, I-80 the northern coast-to-coast interstate, I-55 south to St. Louis, I-57 south to Kankakee and southern Illinois and I-65 to Indianapolis. The I-80, I-90 and I-94 corridor below Lake Michigan is one of the heaviest traveled arteries in the country. There are many more trucks than automobiles. It is literally a truckers' paradise or nightmare. I find it fascinating!

I'm able to hook up with an "18 wheeler" at I-80/90 split with I-94 just east of Gary, Indiana. I carefully follow behind him for over 50 miles through Indiana and Michigan until I have to get off at my exit in Benton Harbor and the Comfort Inn.

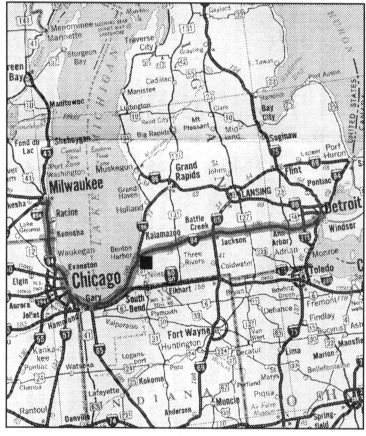

Milwaukee to Detroit via I-94.

CHAPTER XIV

Detroit—Tiger Stadium

It's now Monday morning, August 19th, and I'm headed for Detroit and Tiger Stadium on I-94 east. This is the beginning of the fourth and toughest leg of the journey. I'll serpentine through the northeast by myself covering 10 games in 13 days and some 3,000 miles.

It's a short drive, about 200 miles, from Benton Harbor to Detroit. However, it's raining and I run into bumper-to-bumper traffic several times along the way. The road is generally flat, the scenery is green and lightly wooded. The roads in Michigan are pretty well beaten up due to the harsh winters, as are many of the cars I see on the road. Incidentally, it looks to me as if ninety percent of the cars in this area are American made.

I can now see why they call this area the "Rust Belt of America". Driving into Detroit, on my way to Tiger Stadium, I pass old steel mills, manufacturing plants, refineries and other gray, gloomy looking facilities. As I near the stadium, I'm on Michigan Avenue, the main drag, and find out there isn't a stadium parking lot and all parking is privately owned. I find parking in a tire establishment a few blocks from the stadium.

Tiger Stadium is one of the oldest, perhaps the grand daddy of the major league stadiums. Although this ballpark looks its age, it does have some really good features that you can't find in the modern day stadiums. Constructed in 1912, it is the only ball field that has a double decked bleacher section. It's also one of the few stadiums where the fans are right on top of the action. In fact, the broadcasters are closer to home plate than the middle infielders. It has real grass, and is of course, not symmetrical. The outfield has some unique corners and right center field is 440 feet from home plate. The stadium has recently added a food plaza just outside the stadium but within the confines. There are plans underway to replace this relic with a new downtown stadium before the turn of the century.

The Tigers are one of the original American League franchises commencing in 1901. Since their inception they have won nine pennants and four World Series. Today they compete in the American League's Eastern Division and have not fared well in recent years.

After graduating from college in 1961, I was working at Geigy Chemical in Ardsley, New York, my first full-time job. At this point in time baseball was not a priority for me. I was resigned to playing softball and played for the company team. I also continued with my bowling by participating in two leagues.

At the age of twenty, I volunteered to serve in the New York Army National Guard. About this time my family moved to Bronxville, NY, just north of NYC. We lived on the top floor of a six story apartment building.

This turned out to be quite convenient, because my mother was able to hang a large kitchen towel from our living room window which I could see from the basketball courts where I spent most of my time. This told me that dinner was on the table and I better get my skinny body up there fast or there would be hell to pay!

In 1961, the Washington Senators moved to Bloomington, Minnesota and became the Minnesota Twins. The American League also completed its first expansion since 1901 by adding two new franchises, the California Angels who played in Los Angeles and the "new" Washington Senators.

In 1962, the National League followed by also adding two teams, the "amazing" Mets in New York and the Houston Colt 45's. This resulted in 20 teams for MLB, 10 in each league. They also increased the number of games in the schedule from 154 to 162. This reduced the number of games a team would play each other from 22 to 18. For the start of the 1962 season MLB was aligned as follows:

National League	American League
Chicago Cubs	Baltimore Orioles
Cincinnati Redlegs	Boston Red Sox
Houston Colt 45's	California Angels
Los Angeles Dodgers	Chicago White Sox
Milwaukee Braves	Cleveland Indians
New York Mets	Detroit Tigers
Philadelphia Phillies	Kansas City Athletics
Pittsburgh Pirates	Minnesota Twins
St. Louis Cardinals	New York Yankees
San Francisco Giants	Washington Senators

Tonight, the Tigers host the White Sox, a team I have already seen on three previous occasions during the MLBC. The starting pitchers for tonight's contest are James Baldwin for the Sox and Omar

Olivares for the Tigers. The Tigers score a run in the first on two hits. Olivares is cruising along as he faces and retires the minimum of the first 12 batters. The Tigers add two more runs in the fourth on a Andujar Cedeno two run homer. Olivares completely loses his touch in the sixth by walking four and giving up two hits. When the dust finally settles the White Sox take a 5-3 lead heading into the bottom of the sixth. The Tigers snap right back with four runs, highlighted by a pinch hit three run homer off the bat of Curtis Pride, and regain the lead at 7-5. The score remains that way going into the top of the ninth. The White Sox unload on Detroit's pitchers by scoring seven times aided by two three-run homers. Roberto Hernandez comes in to close out the Tigers in the ninth and preserves a 12-7 Chicago win. When things are going bad, teams find new ways to lose. This loss extends the Tigers' current losing streak to eight games.

This now completes one half of the games. I've attended 14 ball games in 14 different stadiums, covering approximately 7,200 miles in 25 days. The next half will be more difficult from the standpoint of coordinating team schedules and geography. My options are reduced because the number of teams left to visit has become fewer. I'll head back to my motel in Flat Rock which is located in a suburb south of Detroit along I-75.

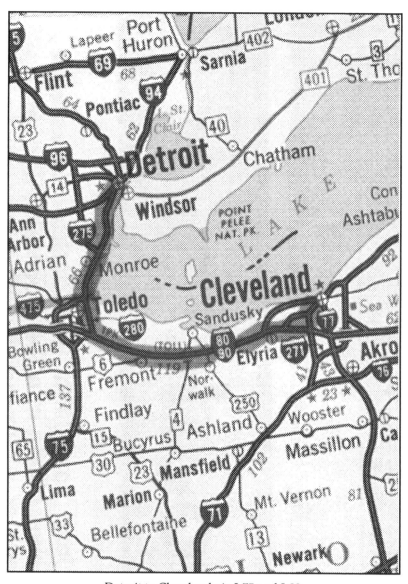

Detroit to Cleveland via I-75 and I-80.

CHAPTER XV

Cleveland—Jacobs Field

From Detroit to Cleveland is an easy day's ride, just about 170 miles around the western edge of Lake Erie. There's quite a bit of road construction at the Michigan-Ohio border, which causes stop and go traffic for about thirty minutes. Once I get to the Ohio Turnpike traffic thins out and moves along at a decent rate. I finally get to my motel at about 4:30 after spending some time shopping. The motel is near the airport in an industrial area, and is just one quarter mile from the RTA train station.

I take the RTA downtown to the Tower City terminal. What a pleasant surprise! The station is just beautiful and leads to the Tower City complex which houses a gorgeous atrium-style shopping mall and food court. It is the most exquisite mall I have ever seen, not because of the shops which are of the usual variety, but due to the unusual ambiance. The mall/rail station is done in marble and brass with dancing fountains that are synchronized to classical music piped-in on a high tech audio system. This is a must see!

The station has a gateway that leads to the Gund Arena (where the Cavaliers' NBA basketball team plays) and Jacobs Field. Jacobs Field is one of the four new ballparks meant to look old. It opened in 1994 and looks beautiful with two levels of seating, a bleacher area in left center field, three levels of suites, a private club pavilion and two restaurants. Prior to 1994, the Indians played in Cleveland Stadium which had the largest seating capacity of baseball stadiums at 74,000.

I had to purchase my ticket well in advance of my MLBC departure, since all home games are sold out very early in the season. The seat I received was in the upper deck in the nosebleed section. At least it was high enough and far enough from the real grass so that my allergies were not a problem. The seats in the stadium are turned to face the action, which you don't find in multi-purpose stadiums.

The Indians franchise is one of the original eight in the American League. They've won a total of three pennants and two World Series over their history. Cleveland won its first American League pennant in 41 years in 1995. The last time they won the pennant was back in 1954 when they won an unprecedented 111 games in an 154 game season. That accolade was short lived as they lost four straight games to my beloved Giants in the World Series that same year. The last time Cleveland won the World Series was 1948, which was the same year that Larry Doby, the first black, entered the junior circuit.

In 1966, at the age of twenty-four, several momentous events occurred in my life. I moved out of my parent's home, I got married, and changed my job, all on the very same day. My wife and I moved to the suburbs—Rockland County on the New Jersey side of the Hudson River, thirty miles northwest of NYC. I immediately joined a softball league and played center field. Many Saturday afternoons I would return home carrying a softball bat and glove on one shoulder, a basketball under one arm and golf clubs strung over the other shoulder. I was not easily domesticated. Sports were the major part of my life and there was not much room for anything else.

In 1966 there were also a few minor changes with MLB franchises. The Braves moved again, this time from Milwaukee to Atlanta, and the California Angels now played in Anaheim next door to Disneyland.

The game between the Indians and the Texas Rangers starts off with a bang in several aspects. First the Rangers send eight batters to the plate in the top of the first inning and score two runs off Cleveland starter Albe Lopez. Then there is *literally* a bang from the thunder which succeeds the lightning that is over the stadium. Well, this all adds up to a one hour and twenty-three minute rain delay. When play finally continues the Indians retaliate with three runs in the bottom of the first, highlighted by an Albert Belle triple off Ranger starter Bobby Witt. The score remains at Cleveland 3, Texas 2, until the fifth inning when both teams score two more runs. In the Indians seventh Manny Ramirez belts a grand slam homer off Texas reliever Jim Russell to give Cleveland a 9-4 lead. Cleveland adds another run on Albert Belle's 41st homer of the season. Eric Plunk and Paul Assenmacher shut down the Rangers the rest of the way and the final score is 10-4. One final note, the Texas Rangers made an error which ended their errorless game streak at 15, a new American League record.

After the game I take the RTA back to the motel. Tomorrow will be a long day as I will drive some 370 miles to Baltimore and then go to the game.

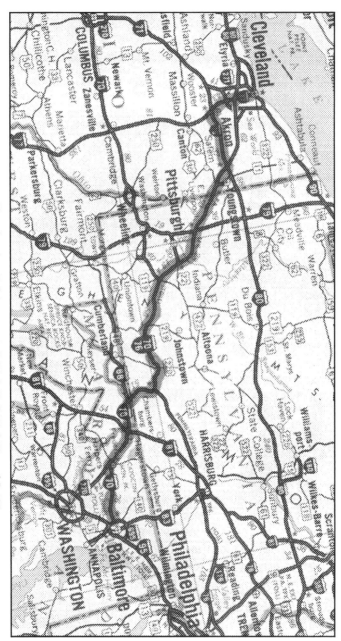

Cleveland to Baltimore via I-77, I-80, I-76, I-70 and I-695.

84

CHAPTER XVI

Baltimore—Oriole Park at Camden Yards

Baltimore lies southeast of Cleveland and it would be helpful to have a navigator on board as it takes a combination of five major interstate highways to get there. It is a very scenic ride as these thoroughfares take me through the Allegheny Mountains in Pennsylvania and the Blue Ridge Mountains in Maryland. This is a beautiful route. It's odd that the roadways in the best condition are free, while the ones in dire need of repair are costly to travel. For example, the Pennsylvania Turnpike, one of the oldest roads in the country, is in horrible condition but costs almost six cents per mile to drive. It takes me five and a half hours to travel the 360 miles to my motel in North Lithicum, a suburb of Baltimore.

The motel is only a quarter of a mile from the light rail station and a twelve minute ride to Oriole Park at Camden Yards. What a great way to go! Both Cleveland and Baltimore have done it right. Good, clean, safe and efficient transportation from the "burbs" to the ballpark. Oriole Park was opened in 1992 and is similar to The Ballpark at Arlington and Jacobs Field. It is a beautiful ball yard, asymmetrical with three decks of seating, pavilion areas and a bleacher section. One of the major sights to be seen here is the old Baltimore & Ohio Railroad warehouse located beyond the right field fence. Many of you might recall the banners hanging from this warehouse that signified Cal Ripken's consecutive games played streak.

As I was on line to get my tickets, I met a couple from Pleasanton, California, just ten miles from my home. They were on a tour of six stadiums: Cincinnati, Cleveland, Baltimore, New York (Yankees), Boston and Montreal.

It's hot and muggy tonight; the humidity is hard to take for a transplanted New Yorker who has gotten real used to California weather. My seats are right behind home plate and about thirty rows up. I happen to be seated right behind the commentator and the technical producer of ESPN's Baseball Tonight show. The stadium is packed for two reasons. First, the Orioles are still bidding for a wild card spot in the playoffs and second, Eddie Murray is just two home runs shy of his 500th.

The Orioles are also one of the original eight American League franchises playing their first and only year (1901) in Milwaukee. They became the St. Louis Browns in 1902 and remained as such for 52 years. In 1954 they became the Baltimore Orioles and have been that ever since. They have won seven pennants and three World Series for their franchise.

From 1966 to 1969 I worked in mid-town Manhattan for Shell Chemical Company. The long tiring commute each work day was interfering with my sports activities. So in June of 1969, I went to work for New York Telephone just across the river in White Plains. I of course immediately joined the softball and bowling teams. At the advanced age of thirty I gave up playing competitive basketball and was assigned to a player/coach role for the company team.

In 1968, the Athletics moved for their second time, this time from Kansas City to Oakland, California. However, this was minuscule to the change that MLB went through in 1969. For starters, both leagues expanded for the second time by adding two teams each. The National League awarded franchises to San Diego and Montreal, Quebec. This was the first time MLB would have regular season play in a country other than the United States. The American League added teams in Seattle and a new franchise in Kansas City.

MLB now had 24 teams, 12 in each league. It was also decided at this time to split each league into two divisions to promote more competition and revenue. Additional revenue was a result of the need for divisional playoffs to determine the league champion. The 162 game schedule was still intact; however, each team played their divisional rivals 18 games a season, while having 12 games against their inter-divisional opponents. This major reorganization resulted in the following structure for the start of the 1969 season:

National League

Eastern Division	Western Division
Chicago Cubs	Atlanta Braves
Montreal Expos	Cincinnati Reds
New York Mets	Houston Astros
Philadelphia Phillies	Los Angeles Dodgers
Pittsburgh Pirates	San Diego Padres
St. Louis Cardinals	San Francisco Giants

American League

Eastern Division	Western Division
Baltimore Orioles	California Angels
Boston Red Sox	Chicago White Sox
Cleveland Indians	Kansas City Royals
Detroit Tigers	Minnesota Twins
New York Yankees	Oakland Athletics
Washington Senators	Seattle Pilots

Tonight's game adds some extra excitement for me. It is the first time I will see the Seattle Mariners and the Baltimore Orioles with Ken Griffey, Jr., Alex Rodriquez and Cal Ripken in person. I am not disappointed. All are spectacular. Rodriquez has two home runs, Ripken has a solo homer as well as three hits and Griffey has a few defensive gems. It is your typical American League affair with 15 runs crossing the plate and a lengthy three hours and fourteen minutes of play. When it is all over the Orioles have a 10-5 victory.

Back on the light rail to my motel. It was a great game, a great ballpark, enthusiastic fans and clean and comfortable transportation—altogether one of the best experiences I have had thus far.

Baltimore to New York via I-95 and I-87

CHAPTER XVII

New York—Yankee Stadium

It's Thursday, August 22nd, day 28 and I have a short drive today to the home of the Yankees and "The House That Ruth Built". It's about 200 miles from Baltimore to New York City, north on Interstate 95. I-95 is the east coast's north-south equivalent to I-5 on the west coast. I-95 runs from Maine to Florida, connecting the major cities of Boston, Providence, New York, Wilmington, Baltimore, Washington DC, Richmond, Savannah, Jacksonville and Miami. Unlike I-95, I-5 goes through the middle of Washington, Oregon and California, mostly farmlands and small towns, and therefore bypasses some of California's major cities, i.e., San Francisco and San Jose. I've taken today's route many times before as my family would travel from New York to Florida a few times each year to visit my grandparents and parents, who had moved there in the fifties and sixties respectively.

I take the Fort McHenry tunnel which passes under the Baltimore harbor and proceed northeast on I-95. There is a lot of industry here with pollution and haze covering the city.

Coming up the New Jersey Turnpike, I see my first view of Manhattan to the east. There is the fabled skyline and it still gives me a thrill. I'll continue up the Jersey side of the Hudson River, crossing the Tappan Zee bridge about thirty miles northwest of New York City and go into Irvington, New York, where I'll stay with my brother and his wife. Tonight my nephew Jonathan and his friend Sarah will accompany me to the game where we will see the Yankees host the California Angels.

Well, here I am back at the place where I began my life. I was born just a long fly ball from Yankee Stadium. My father was hustling in the pool hall across from the stadium all that night till early in the morning. When he got the call that I was about to be born, he dropped his pool cue and ran all the way up the hill to the hospital.

When we talk about the New York Yankees, we are speaking about the most successful franchise in all sports. They have to their credit an impressive 34 American League titles and 23 world championships in their 96 year history.

Yankee Stadium was opened for baseball in 1923. This ballpark abounds with tradition. In 1941, Joe DiMaggio began his record 56 game hitting streak here. In the 1956 World Series, Don Larsen pitched his perfect game at the Stadium. And in 1961, Roger Maris hit his record breaking 61st home run.

The Stadium was completely renovated in the mid 70's to look more like a modern ballpark. The pillars and posts which obstructed views were all removed. The unique nooks and corners were smoothed out and the playing field became more uniform and symmetrical. As you probably know by now, I prefer asymmetrical playing fields. They moved the monuments that were in the field of play in deep center field (461 feet from home plate) to a new location beyond the fences. They took the famous upper deck facade and relocated it to trim the bleacher section. It now looks more like those multipurpose stadiums built in the 1970's than the new ballparks which are made to look old.

In 1972 I went on the disabled list for the second time in my athletic career due to a small hernia problem. While I was gone, the softball team went into a slump. Did they miss me that much or did they simply function better when I was around to nag at them? As for me, I couldn't wait to get back into the swing of things. It took four long unbearably dull weeks, but finally I returned to some cheers and a few moans. They would have to get back to work and I really drove them hard. They responded well and we made some giant strides that season.

In 1969, Seattle received an American League team—the Pilots. However, this franchise was short lived as they moved to Milwaukee in 1970, the very next season, and became the Milwaukee Brewers. In 1972, the "new" Senators were moved again, this time to Arlington, Texas and became the Texas Rangers. The Brewers took the Pilots' place in the American League Western Division in 1970. However, in 1972, when the Senators moved to Texas, the Rangers were placed in the west and the Milwaukee Brewers moved over to the east.

We drive from Irvington, NY to Yankee Stadium, about a 45 minute ride through the west Bronx. My nephew knows just where to park which gives us easy access to and escape from the stadium. By the way, he is a die hard Yankee fan and has been a loyal supporter over the years. Our seats are great, about 25 rows up from home plate. Stadium prices are the highest I've seen yet: $5 for a beer! Bob Sheppard is still the public address announcer. I remember hearing his deep melodious tone when I was just a kid. He's been here about fifty years which is comforting because with all the changes some things are still the same.

And now to game number 17. Chuck Finley gets the starting nod for the Angels and Kenny "the riverboat gambler" Rogers starts for the Bronx Bombers. The Angels get to Rogers with five runs in the top of the first and the New Yorkers are not able to recover from this deficit. Finley cruises to the victory, pitching seven innings and giving up two runs on five hits, which includes a solo home run to Paul O'Neil in the Yankee fourth. The final score is a lopsided 12-3 when it's over. The Yankees seem to be playing like a front running horse who has its tongue hanging out in the stretch. We leave the Stadium to the sounds of "New York, New York" by Old Blue Eyes himself. It's really been a complete New York experience.

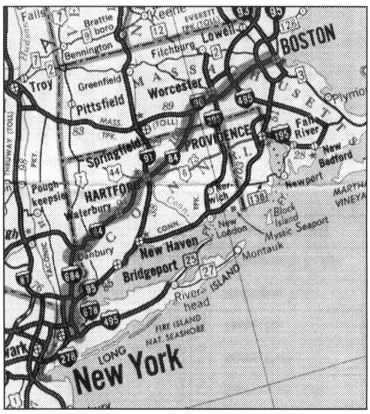

Irvington to Boston via I-287, I-684, I-84 and I-90.

CHAPTER XVIII

Boston—Fenway Park

Boston bound: it's Friday the 23rd of August and day 29 of the MLBC. It is a travel day for my schedule. Although I arrive in Boston in sufficient time to attend the Red Sox night game against Seattle, I prefer to see Fenway for day baseball on Saturday. This will also fit well into my schedule as the Toronto Blue Jays, my next stop, will not be back in town until Monday.

There are several roadways one can use for the 225 mile trip between New York and Boston. Since I have a little more time I will be taking the scenic route via the parkways and Hartford, Connecticut. The speed limit in Connecticut is 55 miles per hour, a restriction difficult to understand as the roads are well paved, generally straight with wide lanes and a median. Coming into Massachusetts, the speed limit immediately increases to 65 miles per hour which makes it a lot easier to make some time and enjoy the beautiful countryside at a more reasonable rate of speed. "Beantown", as it is referred to, is a lot like the city I live near, San Francisco. In fact, I refer to them as sister cities, since they are so alike.

The Red Sox have been in Boston since the beginning of the franchise in 1901. They have won ten pennants and five world championships. Unfortunately, they haven't won a World Series since 1918, which is the second longest dry spell of the original American League clubs. I guess the curse of the "Bambino" still lives on. That is of course the "blunder of a lifetime" decision to trade Babe Ruth to the Yankees who will forever be grateful to the Red Sox.

Fenway Park is one of the three remaining old time ball yards that are still in existence. Built in 1912, the same year that Tiger Stadium was constructed, it shares the distinction as one of the oldest parks still in use today. I've never been to Fenway and I'm anxious to see the "Green Monster" (that's the left field wall) in all its splendor. The movie "Field of Dreams" had some location shots at Fenway. It'll be a treat to see this old monument, especially in the daytime.

I was divorced in 1978 (what woman could compete with my love of sports!) and made another big move: from NY to Northern California where I was near my beloved Giants once again. I had long wanted to live in California and now had the opportunity to move there. I was able to arrange for a job transfer between New York Telephone and Pacific Telephone. This was four years prior to divestiture and it was relatively easy to move between the Bell companies, or as it was called, "Ma Bell" (AT&T).

In 1977, the American League expanded for the third time. This time they added a team in Toronto, Ontario (the second team from Canada) and a new franchise in Seattle. The Toronto Blue Jays played in the Eastern Division while the Seattle Mariners resided in the Western Division. The American League now had 14 teams, seven in each division, and decided to have each team play each other at least 12 times a season. Because of the 162 game schedule, the math works out that some teams needed to play each other 13 times.

I thought it would have been better to cut the season down to 156 games so that the math would work better, but that would have reduced revenues, and that is a no-no. The National League stood pat with 12 teams and hasn't had any changes since 1969.

It's Sunday morning, August 24th, and it's raining. I spent last night in a motel located about twenty miles north of Boston in Woburn. I leave the motel at 11 AM and walk over to the commuter train which takes me into North Station. From there I walk across the street, enter the RTA station and take the Green Line (subway) to Fenway Park. The subway is old and dirty and in dire need of cleaning and painting. I arrive at the Kenmore Station at 12 noon. The RTA is so old that you can't find a straight piece of track in the system and consequently the cars need to be flexible in the middle to negotiate the turns. For this reason they also don't run more than four cars per train.

From the Kenmore Station it's about a half mile walk to the ballpark. The walk along the narrow streets takes me past the street vendors with their pushcarts, cooking and serving any kind of food and drink you can imagine. They offer the likes of hot dogs, hamburgers, sausages, chicken and pizza to name the more popular selections. I can't resist the smell of the Italian sausage, so I grab one on the run. The people just stand on the sidewalks and in the streets and eat and drink. It's one huge tailgate party without a parking lot. I guess the streets are their parking lot.

As I enter the stadium it reminds me more of Tiger Stadium than Wrigley Field. This may have been because it is a gloomy wet day and I saw Wrigley in sunshine. I get to my seat, which is located behind home plate and 30 rows up. The field is still covered with the tarp, but the rain has stopped and they are preparing to remove it. I gaze out at the "Green Monster" and it doesn't look like the looming figure that it appears on television broadcasts. After a half an hour delay due to a wet field, the sun appears and we are ready to play ball! By the way, this is the second ballpark I've attended with a female public address announcer; 3-Com in San Francisco was the first.

The Seattle Mariners send Bob Wells to the mound to oppose Vaughan Eshelman for the Red Sox. The Mariners get on the board in the first inning with an unearned run. In the second, the Red Sox tally three times, including a two run homer by Reggie Jefferson into the right field bleachers, and take a 3-1 lead. The Mariners come right back in the top of the third with two runs to tie the game at 3-3. The game seesaws back-and-forth until the Red Sox sixth, when Darren Braggs delivers a grand slam off Seattle reliever Randy Johnson. This makes the score 9-4 in favor of Boston. The Mariners scratch out another run in the eighth to close out the scoring and the Red Sox come away with a 9-5 victory. The day turns bright and sunny but not for Seattle!

After the game I take the trains back to Woburn and spend a quiet night in the area.

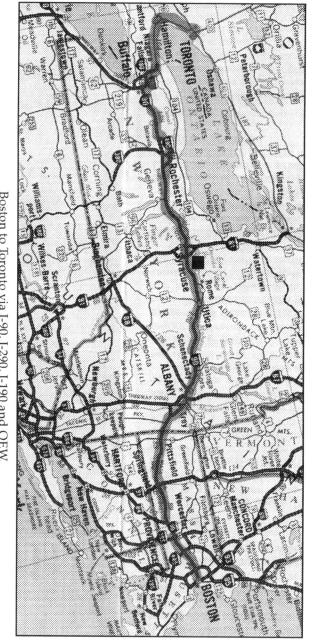

Boston to Toronto via I-90, I-290, I-190 and QEW.

CHARTER XIX

Toronto—SkyDome

It's Sunday, August 25th, and today is a travel day. It is unusual to have a travel day on Sunday, but that's just the way the MLBC schedule works out. From Boston it's due west across Massachusetts and New York on Interstate 90 to Toronto. The Blue Jays don't start their home stand until Monday, August 26th, so I plan to stop for the night somewhere between Syracuse and Rochester, New York.

The day starts out sunny, then clouds up, but now about two hours into my drive it has turned clear and bright. My route goes through some very beautiful countryside both in Massachusetts and upstate New York. About halfway through my drive, I decide to stop outside of Albany for a snack. I also decide to look up a long lost friend and colleague that I worked with some twenty years ago at New York Telephone Company. Fortunately, I find him at home and am able to spend a few memorable hours with him and his wonderful family. This makes for a great afternoon and the remainder of my drive is much more enjoyable. I guess my baseball dream is not only about baseball. I'm finding that some of my detours along the way are just as memorable as the ballparks. By the way, he got gray and I got bald but other than that we found each other unchanged and really enjoyed renewing an old friendship.

I'm spending the night at the Comfort Suites in Vernon, NY. If you can't find Vernon on your map, it is thirty miles east of Syracuse. The hotel is on the same grounds as the Vernon Downs Race Track. My room, which is on the seventh floor, has a spectacular view of the countryside and the race track. Why am I going on about this place in such detail and what's the significance of this? Well, when I was in my late teens and early twenties I spent a lot of my time at the harness tracks in the metropolitan New York City area. On many occasions when studying the racing program, I noticed horses had previously raced at the Vernon Downs track. This is the first time I get to visit Vernon Downs, known to me before only on a racing form. Even though I seem to be cured of some of my bad habits, I am glad they are not racing today and I don't have to test my fortitude. I do manage to feed one of my habits however, and get to an Indian casino which is located very close to my motel.

It's 7:00 AM, Monday, August 26th and I receive my wake up call. I get out of bed and look out my hotel room window to see the standardbreds going through their morning workouts: what a beautiful sight right outside my window! I must confess I spend some time watching the scene and don't start out on my trip to Toronto until about 8:30 in the morning which is a little past my planned departure.

Today I will drive about 275 miles to Toronto and witness game #19: the Blue Jays hosting the Minnesota Twins in the SkyDome. My route will take me past Syracuse, where I spent several years with New York Telephone in the mid 70's; Rochester, where I attended a meeting just two years ago; and Buffalo, which is my entrance to Canada. As I cross through customs at the border, I visit the Canadian side of Niagara Falls. I had seen the US side about twenty-five years ago, but the Canadian side has many more attractions. They have miles of parks, golf courses, botanical gardens, tours of the gorge and many other sights to easily take a week of sight seeing. The horseshoe falls are just magnificent. I drive at least ten miles out of my way and spend about an hour along the gorge before I get back onto the main road to head to Toronto. It was well worth it; the falls are truly an unbelievable sight. The Erie Canal winds back and forth through this part of my drive so I am continually crossing over it. The road in Canada that I am on now is called the QEW, short for Queen Elizabeth Way and it runs adjacent to Lake Ontario. The lake is huge and looks like an ocean with no end in sight. Everything I see around me is so beautiful that it looks like a picture postcard.

Toronto is Canada's second entry into Major League Baseball, the first being Montreal, my next stop. The Blue Jays began in 1977 and were successful early on. They captured two American League pennants and two world championships (1992 and 1993) in their brief existence. The Blue Jays were the first major league team to draw four million fans in a season in 1991. They currently play their home games in the SkyDome which has a 348 room luxury hotel as part of the stadium. In fact seventy rooms have a direct view of the playing field. The SkyDome was ready for the Blue Jays in 1989 and is the only domed stadium with a retractable roof that is opened on nice days and evenings making it possible for the fans to enjoy the game in its natural elements. It is closed for inclement weather which is common in Toronto. It's a twenty minute operation to open or close the roof. The stadium has five levels and accommodates 51,000 people for baseball with three restaurants including a Hard Rock Cafe. The Jumbotron located in center field is enormous.

It is the largest screen in the world and contains over 400,000 individual bulbs. Toronto is an expensive city. The exchange rate is approximately $1.35 Canadian to one US dollar, which appears good for us, but there's little or no benefit for Americans visiting Canada as everything here is priced higher than the states. It has been said that for a family of four to attend a game at the SkyDome it will cost as much as the national debt!

When I left New York to go to my new job in California, I chose to drive across the country. I left on December 3rd, 1978 and made overnight stops in Du Bois, Pennsylvania; Terre Haute, Indiana; Salina, Kansas; Denver, Colorado; and Green River, Utah; before reaching the golden state.

I left Denver on the 7th in a winter snow storm which proved to be a disaster. After successfully driving through the worst part of the Rocky Mountains, I found myself spinning out on black ice and totaling my car. The accident occurred about twenty miles east of Glenwood Springs, Colorado. My car had spun off the road, rolled over several times and wound up on its side next to the Colorado River. I wasn't physically hurt except for a minor cut on my hand from broken glass. The shoulder harness and seat belts saved me from serious injury or even death. I proceeded to pull myself out of the driver's side window and climbed on all fours to the roadway above. It was so slippery on the roadway that I could not stand up without falling over. Fortunately, a good Samaritan in a four wheel drive vehicle picked me up and drove me to the local police station. I got my car towed to Glenwood Springs, where I gathered up all my personal belongings, rented a car and continued on to California.

The roof is closed for tonight's game as it is raining. My seat is on the mezzanine level just behind first base. I watched these same two teams play each other ten days ago in the Metrodome and witnessed an exciting finish. In fact tonight's two starting pitchers, Brad Radke and Juan Guzman were matched up for that game. However, tonight things are different. The Blue Jays score early and often and take a 5-0 lead after five innings. It isn't until the top of the seventh that the Twins push across three runs to make a game of it. However, the Blue Jays bullpen shuts down the Twins in the eighth and ninth to preserve a 5-3 win for Guzman. Although the home team has won, the mood of the crowd is very subdued as the Blue Jays record this year has given them very little to be excited about. Getting out of the SkyDome and parking lots is a bear, and so is the traffic in this city. I finally get on the highway and make my way back to the motel for the night.

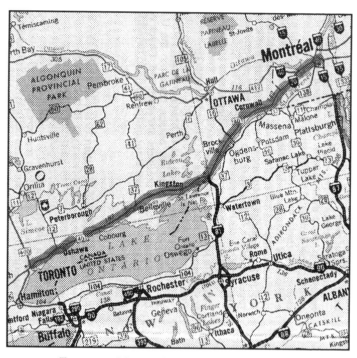

Toronto to Montreal via Hwy 401 and Hwy 20.

CHAPTER XX

Montreal—Olympic Stadium

It's Tuesday, August 27th, and the 340 mile drive between Toronto and Montreal becomes its own MLBC. First the traffic in and around Toronto is the worst I've seen yet. In between trying to interpret the Canadian road signs and scrambling to keep my place on the crowded highways I make a wrong turn, end up getting lost and lose an hour of precious travel time. To add to this dismal picture, it seems as if half the highways in this area are under construction. The weather completes the general fun of this day by being cloudy and rainy with terrible visibility. The route is adjacent to Lake Ontario and then parallels the St. Lawrence River as I get closer to Montreal. I am very happy to finally arrive at my motel, which is close to the Dorval Airport, around 3 PM.

To get to the game I decide to take the Metro, which the hotel provides shuttle service to and from. Once on the Metro, which is very clean and efficient, I meet three young fellows, Eli, Robbie and

Peter, who are kind enough to escort me to the game and act as my tour guides for the evening. Although we are in a largely French speaking city, it is easy for us to communicate as they attend a French/English speaking school. These chaps who are in their mid-teens are real baseball fans. They also are very willing to point out that the Montreal Metro is the largest underground subway system in the world. It's also the cleanest and most attractive rapid rail system I've seen in all my travels. They are extremely proud of their city, their baseball team and their stadium.

As I mentioned earlier, Montreal was the first team outside the United States to obtain a Major League Baseball franchise. The Expos were admitted into the National League in 1969 along with the San Diego Padres. The Expos, unlike their Canadian counterpart in the American League, have not been very fortunate in post season play. They have yet to win a world championship or even a National League pennant. Their best finish was in 1981 when they won the Eastern Division title.

They play in Olympic Stadium, to which a dome has been added in recent years. The dome, which was designed to be removable, is constructed from Kevlar, the material used in bullet-proof vests. A giant crane was built to lift the 65-ton roof off and on, but due to problems with the roof buckling, it does not function in that mode any longer.

In 1979 I was now working for Pacific Telephone and could still compete in softball and bowling. Playing softball was not the same as years before. I was thirty-seven and had lost a step or two in addition to my jump on fly balls. I was unable to handle this decline in my fielding, so I gave it up at the end of the season.

Bowling was another problem. I bowled in one league and it was the top scratch league in Northern California. I was struggling; I couldn't get my average above 185. I tried all three of the bowling balls I had brought out from New York, but had no success. Half-way through the season a league member came up to me and told me I would not be able to score with the equipment I was using. I indicated that I had three different rubber bowling balls for any alley condition. He told me I needed a plastic coated ball for these surfaces. I was fearful of getting a new plastic ball and finding out that my scores would not improve, so I resisted.

The next season I gave in and bought a new plastic ball, a Columbia Yellow Dot. My average jumped to 202 for the next two seasons. The same fellow came to me the following season and convinced me that I now needed a urethane ball. I went out and got a "Hammer" and my average remained in the low 200's.

As we enter the *Stade Olympique* there is a huge food court with just about everything you can think of. My escorts highly recommend that I try the *poutine,* which are french fries with gravy and cheese served in a large cup. It is quite tasty and very filling. We are able to get seats together which are behind home plate and 30 rows up. The stadium has two main seating levels with sky boxes in between. The Jumbotron, although not nearly the size of Toronto's, provides an extremely sharp picture. There are two bleacher type seating areas, one in left field and the other in right, with a totally open area in the center. The dimensions are symmetrical all around. All advertisements are in French; however, the public address announcements are in both French and English.

It is Tommy Lasorda night here in Montreal as the Expos are hosting the Los Angeles Dodgers. Tommy played minor league ball for the Montreal franchise and they are honoring him tonight in light of his recent retirement as field manager. The Dodgers send Hideo Nomo to the mound to face Jeff Fassero, Montreal's ace. The Expos score first with a single run in their half of the third. The Dodgers respond with three in the top of the fourth aided by a Greg Gagne two run homer into the left field bleachers. They add two more in the next inning to take a 5-1 lead. Nomo is able to pitch out of several jams and is helped by poor base running by the Expos. The Dodger bullpen finishes up and shuts down the Expos the rest of the way to preserve a 5-1 victory for Nomo and the Dodgers.

After the game and the Metro ride back to the motel, I bid farewell to my new friends. Tomorrow is a travel day as I will be heading towards Dunkirk, NY, on the way to Pittsburgh and my next game.

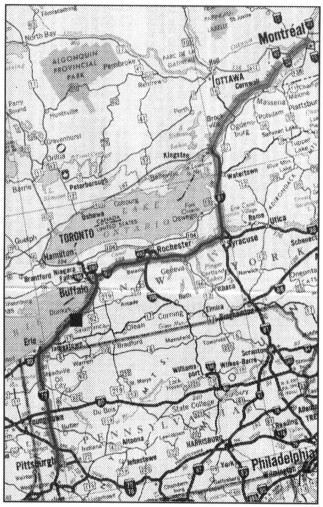

Montreal to Pittsburgh via Hwy 20, Hwy 401, I-81, I-90, I-79 and I-279.

CHAPTER XXI

Pittsburgh—Three Rivers Stadium

It's Wednesday, August 28th, day 34 of the MLBC and I am leaving my hotel in Montreal. I plan to stop early in the evening in Dunkirk, NY, a small town forty miles southwest of Buffalo located on Lake Erie. I prepare for a boring day since the 425 miles I need to cover are mostly on roads I already traveled on just this week.

About ten miles before I reach the Interstate 81 interchange that will take me back to the US, I pass a bus that has a plaque on the side. It reads "Jay Buckley's Baseball Tours, P.O. Box 213, La Crosse, WI. 54602-0213". I drop back and follow the bus. Fortunately, it pulls off at the upcoming rest area which is within three miles. The bus stops and lets the passengers off for a pit stop. I am able to meet Mr. Buckley and share some stories. It turns out that he puts together about 16 tours a year. The one he is currently on is a nine day eight stadium tour which includes Cooperstown. They were in Montreal, at the same time I was, and now they are headed for Toronto and tonight's game in the SkyDome. Mr. Buckley is very interested in my venture and I provide him with a copy of the MLBC itinerary. After our visit I continue on and take the I-81 exit to cross through customs. I am happy to be back in the US and familiar road signs, although I did get used to the Canadian and French Canadian markings and the metric system.

The ride south on I-81 brings back memories of twenty years ago when I was a network planner for New York Telephone Company and this was my territory. I was responsible for 120 central offices in the middle of New York State. The hub of this area was Syracuse and extended south to the Pennsylvania border and north to Canada. Little dots on the map, like Clayton, Alexandria Bay, Gouveneur, etc. come back to life for me. I stop for lunch in a diner outside of Watertown that was one of my favorites when traveling this area.

I continue on I-81 until Syracuse where I transition to and head due west on the New York State Thruway (I-90). I reach Buffalo around 4:30 and make my way into Dunkirk and arrive at 5 PM. The motel that I had made a reservation at turns out to be unacceptable at best. I therefore have to scramble to find another place in an area not known for tourists. This is a working class, blue collar area. Fortunately, I am able to get a room in a very lovely motel right on Lake Erie. I am also able to find a small Chinese take-out restaurant and have a wonderful bowl of Won Ton soup. Later on, this becomes an issue which we will label "the great Won Ton soup search".

The next morning I have a relatively short drive (175 miles) to Pittsburgh. I also luck out because today's game is a late afternoon start at 3 PM which will allow me enough time to check into the motel before proceeding to Three Rivers Stadium. I'm in some new territory here on the Pennsylvania Turnpike. I get to Harmersville, a suburb of Pittsburgh, early in the afternoon and check into my motel. By 2 PM I leave for the ballpark which is a thirty minute drive.

Three Rivers Stadium is aptly named, being at the confluence of the Ohio, Allegheny and Monongahela Rivers. It was built in 1970 on the same site as Exposition Park, the ballpark the Pittsburgh franchise first played in from 1891-1907. In 1908 the Pirates moved into Forbes Field, one of those great old ball fields. It was a great hitters' park with an expansive outfield.

When I was growing up, the Pirates were always the National League doormats. They seemed to always be in the cellar. In fact, prior to 1960 they were the only National League franchise that had not won a pennant since 1927. Then in the 60's they gained respectability by winning the National League pennant and World Series from the New York Yankees, with the likes of Roberto Clemente, Willie Stargell and Bill Mazeroski, to name the more prominent contributors. All-in-all they have won nine pennants and five World Series titles.

Since I gave up softball in the early 80's, bowling was not enough in the way of sports for me. I decided to train for the Bay to Breakers run conducted each year in San Francisco. Here I was raring to go. It was the day before the race and I was visiting with some friends. I had this awful headache and asked my friend for some headache medication. After taking the medication I developed heart palpitations and dizziness. Unbeknownst to me, the headache remedy contained codeine, a drug to which I was allergic. All that training was for naught; I wasn't able to compete in the race the next day. All I had left was bowling.

The traffic getting into the stadium is a bit of a problem. One huge narrow circle around the stadium leads to the parking areas. Once inside the stadium I say to myself, "I've seen this before." It is reminiscent of Riverfront in Cincinnati, and Fulton County in Atlanta. They are all multipurpose circular stadiums with symmetrical dimensions. Fulton County has a slight edge as it has real grass as opposed

111

to the artificial stuff. Three Rivers is a two level stadium with two levels of sky boxes and club seats.

I am in for a treat today as Greg Maddux is pitching for Atlanta. And does he ever pitch! He goes seven full innings, gives no runs on four hits and doesn't walk a batter. The Pirates are able to get two runners on in the seventh with only one out and Maddux slams the door shut by striking out the next two batters. At the end of the seventh the game has consumed just one hour and thirty minutes, vintage Greg Maddux. As you can guess by now the Braves won this one by the score of 5-1.

This game holds two records on my MLBC tour. It had the smallest crowd (12,101 in attendance) and it was played in the shortest amount of time (just two hours and twelve minutes). Even though the crowd was small, getting out of the parking lot was a mess due to the poor access to any major artery. It was also in the heart of the rush hour traffic. I'd hate to think what it would be like with a full house.

I finally get back to my motel at 7 PM. After relaxing for several minutes I decide to get something for dinner, but what? Won-Ton soup sounds good! You see, when my allergies are bothering me, breathing and eating are in competition with each other and hot soup is easy to consume. I drive around for about 45 minutes, gas up the car, find a small Chinese take-out restaurant and have some really good Won-Ton soup.

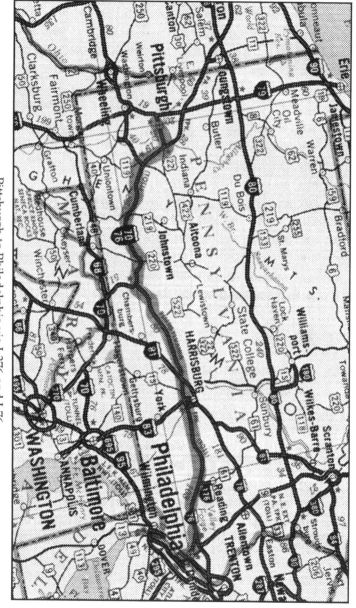

Pittsburgh to Philadelphia via I-376 and I-76.

CHAPTER XXII

Philadelphia—Veterans Stadium

It's Friday, August 30th at 9:07 AM and I'm on my way to "The City of Brotherly Love". It's a beautiful day for the drive, clear and cool, and I can almost smell Fall in the air. About halfway between Pittsburgh and Philadelphia I reach the 10,000 mile point on the MLBC.

I'm just outside Philadelphia as I get to the toll booth. The attendant says, "$11.00, please." I respond, "I don't want to buy the roadway. I just want to use it for awhile." I wouldn't mind paying $11.00 for a highway in good condition, but this turnpike is in desperate need of a renovation. It takes me a total of five hours, including a brief lunch stop, to reach my motel at the Philadelphia airport. After taking care of laundry, getting on the treadmill and a short rest I drive to the Vet. Naturally, I will be rooting for the Phillies as my dislike of the Dodgers will never leave me.

Veterans Stadium was built in 1971 and is the largest of the National League ballparks with a seating capacity around 63,000. It's of the same mold as those other multi-purpose stadiums built in that era. You surely know by now how I feel about them, so I'll spare you the details. However, this place has a few subtle differences I will describe. The park looks a little more open, since the upper deck is essentially uncovered. There is also a great replica of the Liberty Bell on top of the roof in center field. It is illuminated at night and provides the signature for the stadium. The seats are freshly painted in a beautiful shade of deep blue. The best thing about this place is the Phillies' mascot. The Phillie Fanatic is the best mascot in baseball. It is always carrying on with the players, coaches, umpires, ground crew, media and of course the fans. My seat is great, the best so far. I'm sitting eight rows behind the visiting team's dugout and am able to see every pitch, read the lips and catch the facial expressions of the players.

The Philadelphia franchise was one of the National League's original eight. It was established in 1883 and began playing at Recreation Park. In 1938 they moved into Shibe Park (built in 1909) which they shared with the American League franchise Athletics. In later years Shibe Park was renamed Connie Mack Stadium. The Phillies played there until the 1971 season when they moved into Veterans Stadium.

In 1950 the Phillies were known as the "Whiz Kids". They won the National League pennant that year only to lose to the Yankees in the World Series. They had the likes of Richie Ashburn, Curt Simmons and Robin Roberts, to name a few of the standouts. Of the original National League franchises, Philadelphia has won the least number of world championships, just one in 1980, when they defeated the Kansas City Royals. They were also the last team of the original eight to win their first World Series. They do have four National League crowns to their credit.

Other than bowling and an occasional golf game (my worst sport) I was out of sports in the 80's. I had built my own income tax practice from the ground up. This kept me very busy during the tax season and out of trouble for most of the year.

Tonight's pitching match up is Tom Candiotti for the Dodgers against Matt Beech for the Phillies. Both pitchers are in command of their game through the first three innings. The Dodgers get on the board first with a run in their half of the fourth. The Phillies come right back in the bottom of the frame with two runs and take a 2-1 lead after four. The score remains that way until the Dodger sixth when they score five times to regain the lead at 6-2. The Phillies fight back with a single run in the sixth and three more in the seventh to knot the score at 6-6. The score stays tied through extra innings until the top of the twelfth when the Dodgers push across the go ahead run. Todd Worrell, the Dodger closer, shuts down the Phillies to preserve the victory. The star of the night is the Phillie Fanatic. The game takes three hours and fifty minutes, a long tiring night. Coupled with a Dodger victory it makes me more tired and some-what depressed.

Tomorrow I'm off to my old hometown New York for the second time to see the Mets game with my favorite team, the Giants.

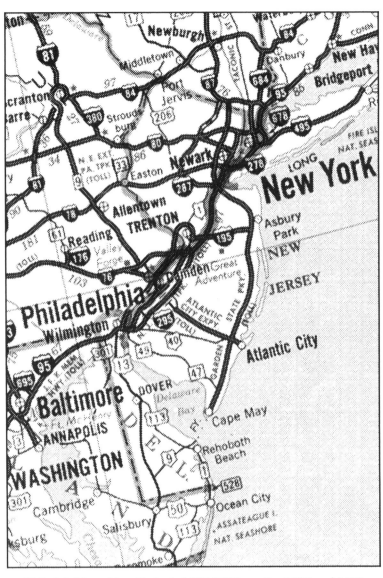

Philadelphia to New York via I-295, NJ Turnpike, I-278 and I-678.

CHAPTER XXIII

New York—Shea Stadium

On to New York again, this time for the "amazing" Mets. It's Saturday morning, the last day of August, and I have a short drive of ninety miles ahead of me, north on the New Jersey Turnpike to Shea Stadium. I will be stopping in Queens, NY to pick up my Aunt Evelyn and take her to the game with me. Since I am very familiar with this area and the roads leading into New York, I decide to travel some new highways.

I'm north of Philadelphia on I-295. This will take me into the New Jersey Turnpike near Trenton, New Jersey. From the Turnpike I cross over into Staten Island, one of the five boroughs of NYC, via the Gothels Bridge. As I pull into the toll plaza the sign reads $4.00, but that's not the bad news. I ask the toll attendant, "How much is the Verrazano Bridge?" That is the bridge connecting Staten Island to

Brooklyn; you know the place where "Dem Bums" used to play. She responds, "It's seven dollars." Sticker shock once again on the east coast.

I begin to see road signs that indicate New York is getting closer and I start to feel the excitement of the City. There is no place in the world like it! I cross into Brooklyn and now it's onto the Shore Line Parkway. This parkway was built after WWII and is in need of a total overhaul. The lanes are extremely narrow and made for mini cars. The cars that travel on this roadway look like bumper cars you find in an amusement park. They all look "dinged up" with different color body parts that are strapped on haphazardly. I pass some old familiar places like Coney Island, Rockaway Beach and Flatbush Avenue. I'm now looking for the Van Wyke Expressway that will take me into Queens. I must be getting close, since I see signs for JFK Airport. Once on the Van Wyke it's a fifteen minute ride to my aunt's apartment. She lives just five minutes from Shea Stadium.

I arrive at my aunt's at 12:30 and we go to the neighborhood diner for lunch. The east coast's answer to the west coast's coffee shops are diners. They have outstanding food, huge portions, moderate prices and an extensive menu selection. They can't be beat!

There is a lot going on in this area today. Besides the Mets game, the US Open tennis tournament is in full swing in Flushing, NY, just a stones throw from Shea. We take a short taxi ride to the Stadium. The weather is absolutely magnificent, about 75 degrees and very low humidity. If I were able to order my kind of weather I couldn't have done any better. I get my time all mixed up and we arrive over an hour before game time. You see, I never change my watch; I leave it set on Pacific Time. Also, contributing to my mix up is that today's game has a 4 PM start as it is the game of the week on Fox television. Thank God it is so beautiful, it doesn't matter.

The Mets came into the National League in 1962 along with the Houston franchise. This was the first time National League baseball returned to the "Big Apple" since the departure of the Giants and Dodgers back in 1957. New York was very hungry for a National League presence and now they had their darling Mets. In their first few seasons the roster mainly consisted of major league stars then in the twilight of their careers. They were even managed by the colorful "Professor" Casey Stengel. They became the laughing stock of baseball with their haphazard play and antics. The loyal fans were very strong-hearted as the Mets would always find a new way to lose a winning or close game in the last inning. My father was one of those die-hard Mets fans. He would actually get sick watching them throw away game after game in the late innings. They would just find a new and creative way to lose. I have never seen him get more aggravated over anything in his life.

However, the "miracle" Mets surprised the sporting world in 1969 when they won the pennant and World Series. They did it with a superb pitching staff that had two "Hall of Famers", Tom Seaver and Nolan Ryan.

For their first two seasons the Mets played their home games in the old Polo Grounds, vacated by the Giants in 1958. In 1964 they moved into their new and current home Shea Stadium. It would be filled to capacity for the return visits of the Giants and Dodgers. It's a five-tier Stadium with a small bleacher area in left center field. There is a huge scoreboard (the largest in the majors) in right center and center field is open to the views of New York City. This openness in the outfield is a very appealing feature that I have not seen in most of the previous ballparks. It breaks up the monotony of seeing stands with seats all around. And if you feel you are bored with the ball game, you can always watch the airplanes as they take off from nearby LaGuardia Airport every few minutes.

The Mets send Robert Person to the mound today to oppose Osvaldo Fernandez of the Giants. The Mets draw first blood by scoring a run in the bottom of the third. The Giants come right back in the top of the fourth to score a run and tie the score at 1-1. Fernandez is forced to leave the game in the fifth when he develops a blister on his pitching hand. The Mets take advantage of the Giant relievers and score six runs in the last four innings and go on to win 7-2. It is a three hour ball game with over 18,000 in attendance.

After the game my aunt and I catch a taxi back to her apartment. I spend a few more hours with her catching up on family happenings. I leave at 10 PM and head for JFK airport to meet my significant other of the last eighteen years. She is flying out from San Francisco and together we will complete the final leg of the MLBC.

I arrive at JFK at 10:30 and as predicted it's a "mad house". I can't find a place to park, so I pull up along side a fence near the Tower Air terminal. Her plane is due at 11:00. Every fifteen minutes the local police drive by and chase the cars away, as it seems to be illegal to park along the fence, although there are no signs to indicate that. After the third chasing, I'm getting really upset and I'm ready to ask the police why they can't find something more important to do like chase real criminals. I'm sure there is no shortage of them in this city. Just then my friend, Judith, appears and we are out of there.

We are now on the road, headed for Irvington, NY. We will be spending the next five days with my brother and sister-in-law before continuing. Before reaching Irvington, we stop in Elmsford (the next town) at a diner for a late snack. We arrive in Irvington at 1 AM and call it a long day.

This now completes leg four and 11,000 miles, 23 ball games and 37 days. Our next game is in St. Louis on September 8th.

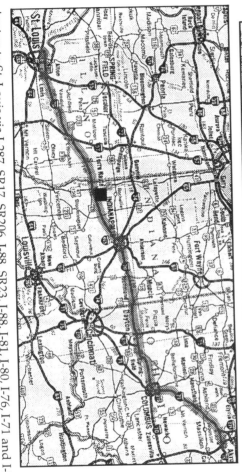

Irvington to St. Louis via I-287, SR17, SR206, I-88, SR23, I-81, I-80, I-76, I-71 and I-70.

CHAPTER XXIV

St. Louis—Busch Stadium

It's Sunday morning, September 1st, and I'm just kicking back today, not thinking about the MLBC. It's Labor Day weekend and I will be spending most of my time with friends and family. The break at this point is very welcomed as the fourth leg has turned out to be thirteen quite grueling days.

The four of us go for a walk and then a ride in this beautiful area of Westchester County, New York. Fall is not quite here yet, but the heat of the summer has mostly disappeared.

On Monday, Labor Day, my brother invites some of his good friends over for a barbecue and stimulating conversation.

Tuesday is a day for chores. I have the car serviced for the cross country trip back to California. I am in desperate need of a hair cut which I am able to accomplish. I had my mail forwarded here so that

I can pay the outstanding bills via the computer. And of course, there is laundry to do.

Well, it's Wednesday morning, September 4th; all the chores are accomplished and we have nothing to do. My brother and sister-in-law are back at work and I'm starting to get antsy and missing travel and baseball. I find a stadium that is not on the schedule, but one we can get to with a slight diversion on the way to St. Louis. So we start heading northwest from Irvington. About four hours later in a light rain we reach our destination and Doubleday Field. It is a very simple charming little field right in the heart of Cooperstown, NY, the home of Baseball's Hall of Fame. There is bleacher type seating all around. However, the home plate seating area is covered with a roof, while the outfield areas are open to the elements. Strangely enough, in this old time setting there is an electronic scoreboard beyond the left field fence.

The Hall is a real treat with lifelike statues of Babe Ruth and Ted Williams welcoming visitors in the immediate entry way. The exhibits are fabulous. This is a must see if you are ever in the area. Cooperstown is somewhat difficult to reach as it is not near any major city or a major highway. Somewhere off a rural road between Syracuse and Albany you'll find this beautiful town that surrounds baseball's tribute to itself. After our visit we drive to Scranton, PA, where we spend the night.

It's Thursday, September 5th, and we are west bound on I-80 which is one of the only two interstates in the country that stretches from ocean to ocean. The other one is I-10 which goes from Los Angeles to Jacksonville, Florida. I refer to I-80 as the "Bridge to Bridge" road as it goes from the Bay Bridge in San Francisco to the George Washington Bridge in New York City.

We plan to stop this evening in Middlesex, which is on Pennsylvania's border with Ohio. Our journey will cover about 300 miles today through the beautiful rolling hills of the Appalachian Mountain range. The weather is cloudy and "coolish" and looks as if it is going to rain at any moment. Hurricane Fran, which is threatening the Carolinas, has started moving onto land and is headed in our direction. So for a good part of the day we are monitoring its progress on the radio. We pass Williamsport, PA, the site of the Little League World Series, where the best teams come from all over the world to play for the championship.

It's Friday, September 6th, and today is another travel day as we make our way to St. Louis. The odometer indicates I have covered exactly 11,500 miles on the MLBC. Today is also the one year anniversary of Cal Ripken's consecutive games played record. In honor of Cal we are driving 400 miles to Terre Haute, Indiana. From Middlesex we are traveling in a west southwesterly direction. The terrain is changing from the hilly country of Ohio to the beginnings of the flat plains of the midwest.

We get into Terre Haute and our motel at 4 PM and ask for a restaurant recommendation. They suggest a small Italian restaurant in a residential area. The food is good, but not spectacular; however, we do meet an interesting couple. The gentleman owns a sports memorabilia store in town and claims to know personally many of the superstars in the sports world. We tell him what we are doing and he offers to put me on the local sports radio show tomorrow. I graciously decline as that would play havoc with the schedule at this point. Maybe I'll ask for his offer again after I finish this book.

Tomorrow it's on to St. Louis and finally a baseball game on Sunday. I'm starting to have withdrawal symptoms as I haven't seen a baseball game in a week. So to partially satisfy my craving for any kind of baseball I will watch Brett Butler's return tonight on television.

This is day 44, September 7th, at 8:55 in the morning and as we are driving we hear that Eddie Murray joined the select group of Willie Mays and Hank Aaron by hitting his 500th home run along with his 3,000 plus base hits. Our drive today is just under 180 miles to

St. Louis. We are now passing through south central Illinois farm lands on I-70. It is hot and muggy, in the 80's for both temperature and humidity. The only low number around is gasoline prices at $1.10 per gallon for unleaded regular.

We arrive by noon at our hotel, which is at the airport. We will catch up on a few essentials and then go out for dinner.

It's Sunday, September 8th, and we're on our way to St. Louis. It starts out overcast and gloomy with rain in the forecast. From our hotel at the airport we hop on the Metro-Link to downtown St. Louis to take in some sightseeing before the game. We visit the Arch, the Mississippi River and the downtown area. The Arch is a magnificent structure and you really can't appreciate how enormous it is until you stand at its base. We also walk into the old Union Station which is now a shopping mall and food court. While walking from the station to Busch Stadium we notice the Bowling Hall of Fame. St. Louis is a very popular sports town and is known as the bowling capital of the world. They also had two major league baseball teams, prior to the St. Louis Browns leaving for Baltimore, and an NBA basketball franchise with the Hawks. They currently have one baseball team, the Cardinals, also a new football franchise, with the relocation of the Rams from Los Angeles, and the Blues NHL hockey team.

The Cards, as the baseball team is referred to, draw fans from all over the midwest. They attract many families which has been excellent for baseball. The franchise began in 1876 and went under several different names through the first 15 years. In 1892 they became the Cardinals and have been that way ever since. The franchise has won a fair share of pennants and World Series titles with 15 and 9 respectively.

They played in Sportsmans Park until the current Busch Stadium was completed in 1966. Yes, this is another of those multi-purpose stadiums built at that time. However, they have completed a major upgrade this season, when they replaced the artificial turf with real grass. I guess this change was instigated when the new football arena for the Rams was built and the field would not have to undergo the abuse it would get from football games. Another distinctive feature is the roof over the upper deck which has cutouts of small arch replicas. Almost all the seats are painted red, which appears on television as a sea of red. However, the first three rows of seats in the lower level are green and I don't know why.

It is Jewish Community Day at the stadium and they are featuring some specialty foods and the added treat of piped-in Jewish music. At a few points during the game the fans are clapping and stamping to *Hava Nagila*.

In 1989 I gave up bowling due to the conflict it was causing with my growing tax practice. Now golf was my only sport and I was awfully frustrated by my lack of competency. I seemed to get worse the more I played. I've taken several series of lessons from time to time but I have never felt comfortable playing golf as I have with all the other sports in which I participated. I just guess I never learned the right technique early on. I continued to play, because I found it very relaxing being outdoors on a beautiful day in a parklike setting. That relaxation was short lived though because eventually I did need to swing at that little white ball. Now I don't mean to tell you that I am a disgrace on the golf course, but scoring in the 90's is not what I call adequate.

Today's game pits Fernando Valenzuela of the Padres against Todd Stottlemyre of the Cardinals. Both pitchers go through the first three innings without a hitch. The Cards rough up Fernando a little in their half of the fourth and push across two runs and take a 2-0 lead. The Padres finally get to Stottlemyre in the sixth and score four times, including a three run homer into the right field mezzanine by Wally Joyner. Valenzuela regains his early form and pitches three more scoreless innings before being lifted in the eighth. The Padres add an insurance run in the ninth to extend their lead to 5-2.

The Padres bring in their closer Trevor Hoffman to finish up. Hoffman starts off very shaky by giving up a lead off single to Brian Jordan followed by a two run blast into the left field pavilion by Gary Gaetti. Hoffman is then able to gather himself and shut the door on the Cardinals and preserve a Padre 5-4 victory. That insurance run in the ninth proved to be the difference in today's ball game.

After the game we head back to the hotel. I convince my companion to ask the concierge to recommend a Chinese restaurant where they serve good Won-Ton soup. He recommends a Chinese buffet restaurant that has "Won-Ton soup you could die for," about twenty minutes away. We find this place and have one of the worst meals we have ever had—so much for local recommendations! We later spend a few unprofitable hours on a riverboat casino on the Missouri River at St. Charles, MO.

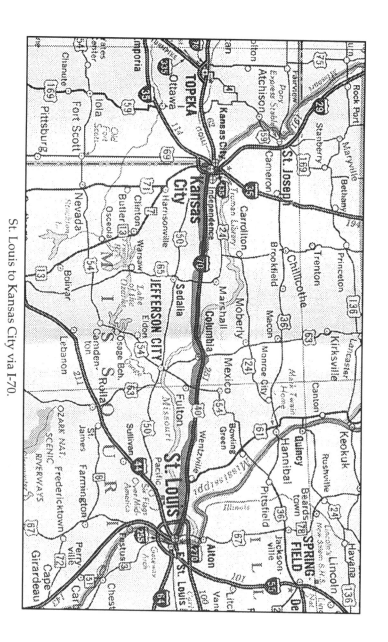

St. Louis to Kansas City via I-70.

CHAPTER XXV

Kansas City—Kauffman Stadium

Monday, September 9th, is a travel day across the state of Missouri. It's an easy day's drive (250 miles) across Interstate 70 from St. Louis to Kansas City. The countryside is beautiful with gently rolling rocky hills and forests of green intermingling. As we approach Kansas City the landscape is starting to level off, a hint of what is to come when we enter the flatlands of Kansas.

The Royals do not open their home stand until the 10th so we won't be attending a game this evening. However, we hook up with friends we knew back in California for dinner and good conversation.

The Royals came into the majors as an expansion team in 1969 along with the Seattle Pilots, now known as the Milwaukee Brewers. Kansas City was home for the Athletics from 1955 through 1967 when they moved from Philadelphia and before they left for Oakland. The city and the Royals have two pennants and one world championship to their credit. That series, in 1985, is referred to as the I-70 series as it was between St. Louis and Kansas City.

I retired from Pacific Bell at the end of 1991, and immediately went to work for the telephone company's major supplier, Northern Telecom. My new office was within a half mile from my previous employment. After commuting to San Ramon for eight years from the San Francisco peninsula, I decided to move to the East Bay and now live within two miles of my work.

For 5 years between 1989 and 1994 I had not bowled. I finally returned by entering a mixed handicap league on the company team in the fall of 1994. I came back surprisingly strong with a lot of my old stuff intact: 200 average for the season. At the age of fifty-two I could still hold my own with most of them and it made my middle-aged heart very glad. Because inside, I was still that little kid banging the ball against the courtyard walls and getting into trouble with Mrs. Davis.

In 1993, the National League finally caught up with its junior circuit, the American League, by awarding two new franchises. The Florida Marlins joined the Eastern Division while the Colorado Rockies were placed in the west. MLB now had its full compliment of 28 teams.

Also in 1993, my Giants lost the West Division title to the Atlanta Braves on the last day of the regular season. The Giants were beaten by "Dem Bums" while the Braves were defeating the expansion Colorado Rockies. All-in-all it was a great season for the Giants as they won more than 100 games.

In 1994, MLB decided to reorganize and realign from two divisions in each league to three. However, they kept the 162 game schedule and followed the pattern set by the American League back in 1977 with each team playing one another essentially the same number of times. I would have preferred more intra-divisional play and less inter-divisional. The 1994 alignment was as follows, although the season was wasted by the strike which shut down the game prior to the end of the season:

National League

Eastern Division	Central Division	Western Division
Atlanta Braves	Chicago Cubs	Colorado Rockies
Florida Marlins	Cincinnati Reds	LA Dodgers
Montreal Expos	Houston Astros	San Diego Padres
New York Mets	Pittsburgh Pirates	SF Giants
Philadelphia Phillies	St. Louis Cardinals	

American League

Eastern Division	Central Division	Western Division
Baltimore Orioles	Chicago White Sox	California Angels
Boston Red Sox	Cleveland Indians	Oakland Athletics
Detroit Tigers	Kansas City Royals	Seattle Mariners
New York Yankees	Milwaukee Brewers	Texas Rangers
Toronto Blue Jays	Minnesota Twins	

We spend Tuesday, September 10th, relaxing and shopping. We look for a good bowl of Won-Ton soup and find a Chinese restaurant that tells us they've got great soup. They don't and we are forced to continue looking in our ongoing search for the great Won-Ton soup.

It's early evening and we are off to have dinner with a different set of friends in the area. After dinner the four of us head out to Kauffman Stadium. The Stadium is right off Interstate 70 and there's lots of parking available. The baseball stadium and football stadium (Arrowhead Stadium) are right next to each other which forms the Harry S. Truman Sports Complex.

Kauffman Stadium is the most attractive looking stadium I've seen thus far. Completed in 1973, it is considered by the players as the best ball park in the majors. It is a three level stadium with sky boxes set back on the second level. There is no bleacher area as the outfield is open and has waterfalls and dancing fountains, a huge scoreboard and Jumbotron which are the prominent parts of its beauty. We are able to look out at the interstate and countryside from our seats behind home plate. They have installed real grass which adds to the ambiance. The only knock I have is the orange-colored seats. They just don't fit into this otherwise gorgeous setting. Prior to Kauffman Stadium the Royals played their home games at Municipal Stadium for the first four years of their existence.

The Royals are hosting the Seattle Mariners tonight as they send rookie pitcher Jose Rosado to the mound to face Seattle's Solomon Torres. The Royals get two runs in the second with a leadoff double and two productive outs followed by two more hits. The score remains 2-0 in favor of the Royals through five innings. In the top half of the sixth, Edgar Martinez takes a Jose Rosado fastball and parks it over the left field fence for a two run homer which knots the score at 2-2. It doesn't stay that way for long as Bob Hamelin drives a Solomon Torres fastball well over the center field fence for a two run blast and gives the Royals back their two run lead at 4-2. Rosado is finished after seven strong innings of work and the Royals bullpen finishes up by pitching scoreless eighth and ninth innings.

The Kansas City fans aren't very enthusiastic as they need to be pushed to cheer. Of course the fact that their team has no chance to compete in the playoffs is affecting their behavior. We have easy access to the freeway which is another good feature of this ballpark and are back in our motel within a half hour. Tomorrow is a travel day as we will make our way towards Denver and our next game on the 12th between the Braves and Rockies.

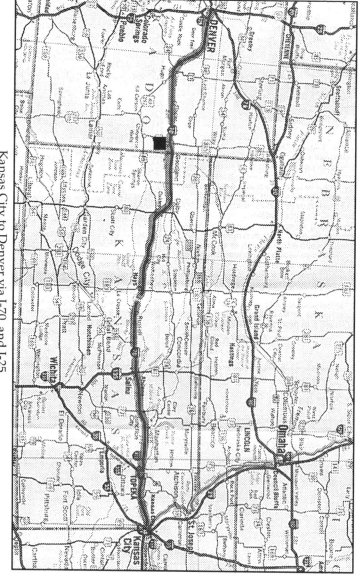

Kansas City to Denver via I-70, and I-25.

CHAPTER XXVI

Denver—Coors Field

It's Wednesday, September 11th, and we're on our way through Kansas and the land of Dorothy and The Wizard of Oz, to the mountains of Colorado and the land of baseballs flying over the fences at Coors Field at a record pace. This will be a two day haul from Kansas City and about 600 miles.

The gently rolling tree studded hills of western Missouri soon turn into flat treeless plains in central and western Kansas. They call this area the high plains. Indeed, as we pull into Burlington, Colorado, just over the state line, we discover that we are at an altitude of 4,100 feet, have gained another hour and are now in Mountain Daylight Time. The weather has finally turned cool tonight so we cut down on the air conditioning and sleep peacefully under a couple of blankets after a long day on the road.

It's Thursday morning, the 12th of September and we have a short 175 mile ride into Denver and a day game at Coors Field. Fall has arrived, it's quite cool out and we have the heater on for the first time since the start of the MLBC in San Francisco. The high plains last all the way to Denver. We reach our motel just south of the city in plenty of time. It takes us just over two hours due to the 75 mile per hour speed limit in Colorado.

It is interesting that although I-70 is the main route between St. Louis, Kansas City and Denver, not to mention the smaller cities along the way, there's still a very small amount of traffic. We didn't encounter any significant traffic until we were in Denver proper. We don't know why this is but it sure beats the big city stop and go in Denver... BIG TIME!

The 1993 expansion Colorado Rockies are one of baseball's greatest success stories. Hungry for baseball, Colorado fans have enthusiastically supported their team with attendance averaging over 50,000 per game even in the 1994 abbreviated season. You can't discount their enthusiasm for football; the Broncos have also played their games to very crowded stadiums and wildly enthusiastic fans. The team rewarded their loyal fans with post season play in the 1995 season, although they didn't get past the first round.

Well, one season of bowling proved to be enough for my ego. Anyway we couldn't put together a company team the next season. There weren't enough employees willing to make the necessary commitment to the long bowling season. Again I was left with just golf. This time I signed up for a weekend golf school. We hit about 600 balls each day for two days. I was able to hit my five iron pretty consistently at the range. However, that didn't last long. When you're on the course for the real deal, all the lessons seem to be a big blur.

The Rockies played their first two seasons in Mile High Stadium, home of the Denver Broncos NFL team. The stadium converts from football to baseball by floating back the entire east stands to form an asymmetrical baseball field. In 1995 they moved into the newly constructed Coors Field located in the LODO (lower downtown) area of Denver. They have completely renovated the old industrial area and turned it into upscale shops, restaurants and living space.

The stadium is a breed of the new meant-to-look-old ballparks. It's a tri-level stadium with luxury suites above the club (second) level. There is ample bleacher seating in left and left center fields. And then there is the Rock Pile, which is bleacher seating well above the center field wall, nosebleed territory. The Rock Pile is so high that no one has hit a baseball into it as yet. There are purple colored seats in the upper deck indicating the mile high elevation mark.

You can walk completely around the stadium on the pavilion and never lose sight of the game. This is similar to what they did at Oriole Park at Camden Yards and the new Comiskey in Chicago. The fans in Denver are very proud of their new stadium and think it's the best in baseball.

The Rockies enter today's game on a four game winning streak and two straight over the Braves. Atlanta sends their ace John Smoltz to the mound to oppose Roger Bailey of the Rockies. Both pitchers get off to a shaky start by giving up three run homers in the first inning. Ryan Klesko hits his homer over the 375 foot sign in right center field, while Ellis Burks hits his three run blast into the left center field bleachers. The Rockies continue their assault on Smoltz by scoring three more runs in the second to take a 6-3 lead. The Braves peck away at Roger Bailey by scoring single runs in the third and fourth innings and then deliver the knockout blow in the fifth when Fred McGriff hits a two run blast into the right field pavilion giving Atlanta a 7-6 lead. The Rockies get to Smoltz again in the sixth with three more runs and regain the lead at 9-7. Both starters are gone by the start of the seventh and the Braves draw within one run by adding one in that frame and now trail 9-8. The Rockies continue their assault on the Braves' pitchers by scoring three in the seventh and four in the eighth to put this one out of reach by taking a commanding 16-8 lead.

Ellis Burks becomes the first Rockie ever to reach the 30/30 mark with 30 home runs and 30 stolen bases. During the eighth and ninth innings the game was played during a lightning and thunderstorm, but it didn't dampen the enthusiasm of the Rockies' fans as they stayed through the game to its conclusion. After the game we spend some time with a fellow "dreamer" from Denver reminiscing about baseball.

We have dinner at a Chinese restaurant near the motel and enjoy a fairly decent bowl of Won-Ton soup and more. But it's just not that great flavor I enjoyed so much at the take-out in Dunkirk, New York. The great Won-Ton search continues! For the next four days we will be making our way towards Seattle and game #27.

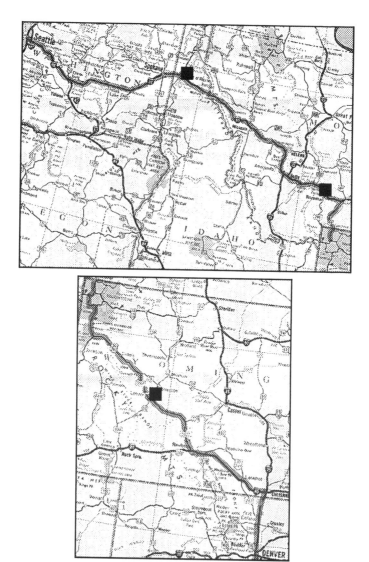

Denver to Seattle via I-25, I-80, US 287, US 89 and I-90.

CHAPTER XXVII

Seattle—King Dome

Today is the 50th day of the MLBC and Friday the 13th to boot. It's a long haul between Denver and Seattle, about 1,300 miles. We will take it easy since the Mariners do not start their home stand until Monday night the 16th.

We leave Denver during the morning rush hour. Traffic seems as bad as the Bay Area. Provisions have not yet been made for the explosive growth and resultant traffic problems. There is one north-south freeway, no car pool lanes and no rapid transit/light rail system. It's a very attractive city but the congestion is beginning to take its toll.

As we reach the outskirts, the traffic thins considerably and we sail along north on I-25 into Wyoming. On all our trips to this state, the wind has always blown at a fairly respectable rate, to put it mildly, and this time is no exception. At Cheyenne we take I-80 westbound to

Rawlins where we pick up US 287 northwest to Lander and our final stop for the evening. We begin to cross the Continental Divide which snakes around the highway for many miles. By the time we reach western Montana we will have crossed it five times. Lander is a surprise. After hours of flat "deserty" arid plains we discover this little town of about 7,000 people in the Lander Valley of Wyoming which locals call Wind River Country. A river does run through it and it looks prosperous and thriving. Voted one of the five best small towns in the country in 1993, it would certainly receive our vote. Of course the whole region is suffering from the drought which has affected the western states badly this summer. We have some laundry to do and then to bed.

It's Saturday, September 14th, the odometer reads 13,546 miles and we are just leaving Lander to continue our way northwest. Our route takes us through the largest park thus far. It has an infinite number of levels with numerous sky boxes and no luxury suites. The park is beautifully decorated with aspens, evergreens and pines. Today's game pits the Tourists against Old Faithful the host team. At 1:30 PM MDT Old Faithful brings in their "Closer" who finishes the game in a spectacular fashion. The final stats for today's game are as follows:

Final Score: Old Faithful 1, Tourists 0

Home Runs: One

Attendance: Approximately 3,000

Time: A snappy 3 minutes and 20 seconds

Temperature: 52 degrees

Losing Pitcher: Too many to list

Winning Pitcher: Yellowstone National Park

The Park took a real big hit in 1988 when fire devastated a major portion of its forests. Blackened gray sticks that used to be trees now stand bare against the sky. We leave Yellowstone through the north gate which brings us into Montana. The first thing we notice is the speed limit signs. There is no speed limit; the sign reads, "Prudent and Reasonable". What a unique approach! However, due to the climbs and sudden curves, at times "Prudent and Reasonable" becomes "Downright Dangerous". We complete our days' travel in Bozeman.

It's Sunday, September 15th, and another travel day. We leave Bozeman at 8:30 on a beautiful fresh cool morning. There are rain showers throughout the area and we pass in and out of them as we travel west bound along I-90. The scenery shifts within minutes from fertile valleys of ranches and farms to heavily wooded pine covered Rocky Mountain terrain. Crossing the Continental Divide for the last time, we descend into Butte from the high sierra country to barren treeless prairie in no more than five minutes. We finish our day in the Idaho panhandle at Post Falls and gain another hour, putting us finally in our home time zone. Tomorrow we will travel across the state of Washington and wind up in Seattle for a Monday night baseball game.

We leave Post Falls about 8 AM. The sky is clear and the day cool and sparkling bright after a fairly good rain the night before. We are able to make good time with the roads in great shape and the 70 MPH speed limit. Eastern Washington has high plains and lots of wheat growing areas. We cross the Columbia River and immediately climb to over 2,500 feet. The surrounding land grows steeper and more forested. We enter the Cascades which have some of the most beautiful scenery seen on the trip. After crossing the Cascades we descend into the Seattle area and our destination near the airport.

We get to our motel early enough to use the exercise room, clean up a bit and drop my laptop, which shattered the screen. This last event was somewhat traumatic as you can probably guess. Some time was spent in seeking a solution to this problem by either purchasing a new laptop or repairing the old one. In either case we will get an answer to this problem tomorrow when we go back to the local shop.

In 1969, Seattle won the rights to an expansion team called the Pilots. They promptly moved to Milwaukee the very next year and were renamed the Brewers. Seattle did not get another American League franchise until the Mariners in 1977.

The franchise had not been successful in getting into post season play until 1995 when they won the American League Western Division's crown. Their divisional playoff series against the New York Yankees was one of the most exciting series ever played. They defeated the Yankees in the final game and went on to the American League Championship Series where they lost to the Cleveland Indians.

They are blessed with three of the brightest stars in baseball today, Ken Griffey Jr., Alex Rodriquez and pitcher Randy Johnson. These three should be able to keep the Mariners competitive for many years.

Since sports seemed to fade from my life, I needed something to fill the void. What we have been doing for the last four years is take vacations that require long car trips. Nothing like this 15,000 mile journey, but six to ten trips that cover 2,000 to 2,500 miles. We get to see a lot of this great land that way. It's really a lot different from what you see on either coast.

We meet an old friend for dinner, who recently moved to Seattle, and then drive to the King Dome. Traffic and parking are difficult at best. The King Dome has three levels with sky boxes between the first and second. There is a huge scoreboard and Jumbotron in left field. The place is packed for tonight's game with the Rangers, as the Mariners are in a battle for a post season playoff berth.

The Rangers send John Burkett to the mound to face the Mariners' Jamie Moyer. The Mariners get off to a fast start by scoring two runs in the first and take a 2-0 lead. As it turns out, that is all the runs they need as Moyer pitches eight scoreless innings and Bobby Ayala completes the shutout by pitching a scoreless ninth.

The crowd at the King Dome was ecstatic from the first pitch to the last as they cheered their Mariners on to victory. They even stood up and cheered after the Rangers had two outs in each inning. The attendance was the largest I've witnessed at 50,544.

A late note: Paul Molitor got his 3,000th hit in Kansas City tonight and became the 20th major leaguer to attain this feat.

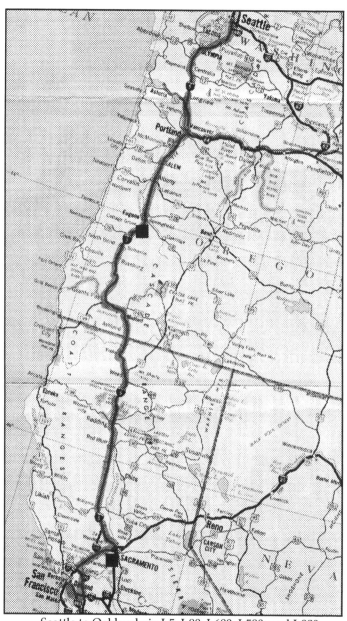

Seattle to Oakland via I-5, I-80, I-680, I-580, and I-880

CHAPTER XXVIII

Oakland—Alameda Coliseum

It's Tuesday, September 17th, and day 54 and this is the final segment, about 800 miles straight south on Interstate 5. The Athletics do not get home until the 23rd, so we have plenty of time to get there. After spending several unsuccessful hours in the computer store, it is determined that my laptop is beyond repair. We finally get on the road at 1 PM and make our way south.

We stop for dinner at our favorite Portland eatery and then get back on the road and travel another 120 miles to Cottage Grove, Oregon where we spend the night.

It's Wednesday and we will drive about 500 miles to Judith's place in Sacramento. It is a beautiful day and seeing Mount Shasta loom over the highway for miles and miles is a sight to behold. Although we have seen this magnificent mountain many times before, it is always as if it were the first time. While listening to the radio, we hear that Dodger hurler Hideo Nomo pitched a no-hitter last night. We arrive in Sacramento at 5 PM. We will spend the night here before I head for home tomorrow morning.

It's day 56, September 19th, and I'm finally on my way home. It is only eighty-five miles from Sacramento to my house, but it takes me over two hours. I run into bumper-to-bumper traffic for the last twenty miles. Yes, I admit the Bay Area traffic is the worst I came across, but that's the price you pay to live in this great area of the country. It takes me over twelve hours to unload the car and put my things away, but remember, two months away from home is a long time.

On Friday, September 20th, I return the car to the rental agency. I totaled 15,082 miles in 56 days. That averages out to 269 miles per day. I start to get my finances back in shape, as well as my back, as I make a visit to my Chiropractor. I get a few staples for my empty refrigerator and start my garaged automobiles. I also look into my laptop computer problem and think I may have found a solution.

It's Saturday and I get just about everything taken care of and back in order. In case you were wondering, the lump below my knee has finally diminished and looks and feels just about normal. I go into the office for several hours and pull up the 36 E-mails that are stored in my mail box. I go for a haircut and then to the market to restock the cupboard. The mail that was temporarily forwarded to my parents' home arrives in the afternoon. Between getting the box of mail cared for and the laundry done, it causes another very late night.

On Sunday, I spend most of the day taking it easy. However, I do get out to hit a small bucket of golf balls and watch the second half of the 49ers game. In the evening I go to another domed stadium. This one is in San Jose. It is quite small in comparison to the others I've been to. This one has one level of seating with a capacity of under 1,000. There are no sky boxes or luxury suites. This stadium is called Temple Emanuel.

It's Monday, September 23rd, day 60, game 28 and this is the finalé, the final act. I leave my home at 5 PM. It is about 75 degrees as opposed to two months ago when I departed for my first game in San Francisco when it was 97 degrees. I am prepared for the Oakland climate as I am wearing a sweat shirt and carrying a warm jacket. Oakland does not experience the fog and moist cold air of San Francisco, but it does cool down due to the prevailing winds of the Pacific coast.

The Athletics franchise began at the turn of the century as the Philadelphia Athletics. They then moved to Kansas City for 13 years between 1955 and 1967. In 1968 they arrived in Oakland where they have been ever since. They share Bay Area baseball with my San Francisco Giants. Candlestick Park and the Oakland Coliseum are about seven miles apart as the crow flies. The A's as they are now dubbed have won their share of post season titles, all of them coming from either Philadelphia or Oakland with a total of 15 pennants and 9 world championships. They have also had their fair share of "Hall of Famers"—the likes of Reggie Jackson and Jim (Cat Fish) Hunter to name the more prominent.

Well, what am I doing with myself today? Today I am planning for this crazy idea I have to attend a baseball game in each of the 28 stadiums. Have you ever heard of such nonsense? In fact this nut is going to do it by car. It will take two whole months and means traveling some 15,000 miles in the dog days of summer. Sitting at the dining room table for hours and days poring over team schedules and road maps and then planning to write a book about the trip and my life. Who in their right mind would want to read such a boring story about a kid growing up in the Bronx who's decided to serpentine across America?

I arrive at the Oakland Alameda Coliseum at 6:05. It was just renovated for the return of the Oakland Raiders NFL franchise. It has three levels of seating areas with sky boxes just below the third level. In the outfield where the renovation took place, it has two small bleacher seating areas, one in left center and the other in right center. There are mezzanine seats above the bleachers and luxury suites above the mezzanine level and finally stadium seating high above the luxury suites. From the mezzanine upward the seating is for football as it is out of the range for baseball viewing. There are two large scoreboards and Jumbotrons, one on top of the left field stands and the other duplicated on top of the right field stands. The outfield grass is pretty chewed up since the Raiders played a football game here just yesterday.

For the final game of my baseball dream, the Texas Rangers send Bobby Witt to the mound to face John Wasdin of the A's. Each team is able to put runs on the board early and often. At the end of the second inning, which took one hour to complete, the A's hold a 4-2 lead. After that scoring spurt the game settles down with each team scoring just one run in the remaining innings. It's cold but not as bad as "Comdlestick" Park. The two ballparks in the San Francisco Bay Area were the only ones where I needed to wear a long-sleeved shirt; in fact, it was a minimum of a sweat shirt in each.

I am now on my way back home and reflecting on all I have just accomplished.

CONCLUSION

So there it is. I have done what I set out to do. I traveled many miles, 15,123 to be exact and slept in many motel rooms, so many that they all seem to blur into one. I have passed through thirty two states and two countries. I have seen 28 ball games in 60 days. I have eaten many different kinds of food, some very good and some very bad, including searching for the perfect Won-Ton soup which I may have found in a tiny little town in the northwest corner of New York State. I have lived out of one suitcase and one Dodge Intrepid. I have met lots of people, driven through hundreds of cities, and I have fulfilled my dream. Right now I'm sad it's over. Would I do it again? You bet ya!

What has come out of this? Years from now when I look back on this "odyssey", what great thoughts and insights will I have—what conclusions?

My certainty is that this great game of baseball will survive. It will last in spite of the lawyers, agents and arbitrators who want to control and destroy its spirit, the players who have lost their identity and dedication and who will change teams for the almighty buck, as quickly it seems as they change their underwear, and the owners who lack integrity and are easily lured to move their franchise to cities where the big dollars are offered. Fans are held hostage: do they follow their favorite players or do they root for and support their local team?

But, in spite of all this, the game will survive because baseball is part of our past. It reminds us of what was good and what can be good again. Baseball is the best of America and the best of us.